REFERENCE USE ONLY

D0574400

REFERENCE USE ONLY

EYEWITNESS VISUAL DICTIONARIES

THE VISUAL
DICTIONARY *of the*
EARTH

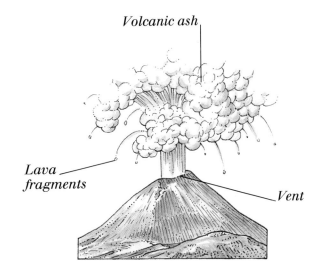

Volcanic ash

Lava fragments

Vent

ACTIVE VOLCANO

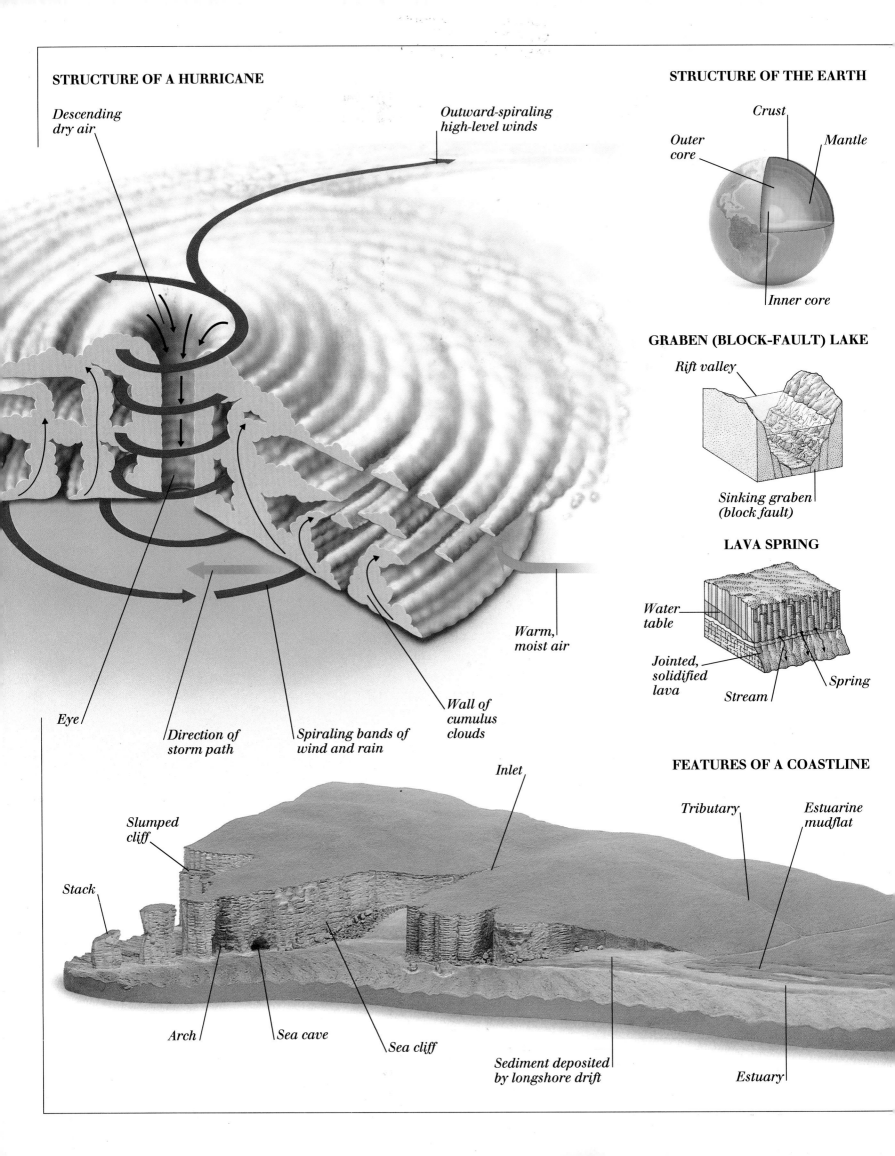

STRUCTURE OF A HURRICANE

Descending dry air

Outward-spiraling high-level winds

Warm, moist air

Eye

Direction of storm path

Spiraling bands of wind and rain

Wall of cumulus clouds

STRUCTURE OF THE EARTH

Outer core

Crust

Mantle

Inner core

GRABEN (BLOCK-FAULT) LAKE

Rift valley

Sinking graben (block fault)

LAVA SPRING

Water table

Jointed, solidified lava

Stream

Spring

FEATURES OF A COASTLINE

Inlet

Tributary

Estuarine mudflat

Slumped cliff

Stack

Arch

Sea cave

Sea cliff

Sediment deposited by longshore drift

Estuary

YOLO COUNTY LIBRARY
226 BUCKEYE STREET
WOODLAND, CA 95695-2600

THE VISUAL
DICTIONARY *of the*
EARTH

REF
J550.13
VIS

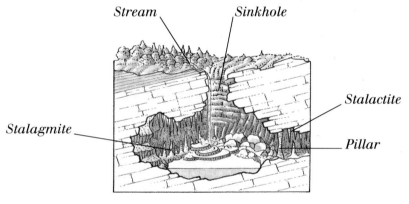

Stream   *Sinkhole*

Stalactite

Stalagmite   *Pillar*

CAVE

Headland

Remnants of former headland

DORLING KINDERSLEY

LONDON • NEW YORK • STUTTGART

A DORLING KINDERSLEY BOOK

PROJECT ART EDITOR JOHNNY PAU
DESIGNER PAUL CALVER

PROJECT EDITOR GEOFFREY STALKER
CONSULTANT EDITOR MARTYN BRAMWELL
U.S. EDITOR CHARLES A. WILLS
U.S. CONSULTANT PROFESSOR WARREN YASSO

MANAGING ART EDITOR PHILIP GILDERDALE
SENIOR EDITOR MARTYN PAGE
MANAGING EDITOR RUTH MIDGLEY

PHOTOGRAPHY ANNA HODGSON, ANDY CRAWFORD
ILLUSTRATIONS COLIN ROSE, JOHN TEMPERTON

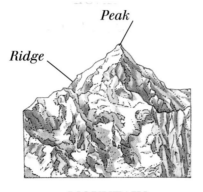

Peak

Ridge

MOUNTAIN

Rossby wave *Rossby wave becomes more developed* *Fully developed Rossby wave*

FORMATION OF ROSSBY WAVE IN THE JET STREAM

Water vapor forms clouds

Water evaporates from sea

River flows into sea

FIRST AMERICAN EDITION, 1993

2 4 6 8 10 9 7 5 3 1

PUBLISHED IN THE UNITED STATES BY
DORLING KINDERSLEY, INC., 232 MADISON AVENUE
NEW YORK, NEW YORK 10016

COPYRIGHT © 1993 DORLING KINDERSLEY LIMITED, LONDON

ALL RIGHTS RESERVED UNDER INTERNATIONAL AND PAN-AMERICAN COPYRIGHT CONVENTIONS.
NO PART OF THIS PUBLICATION MAY BE REPRODUCED, STORED IN A RETRIEVAL SYSTEM, OR TRANSMITTED
IN ANY FORM OR BY ANY MEANS, ELECTRONIC, MECHANICAL, PHOTOCOPYING, RECORDING, OR OTHERWISE,
WITHOUT THE PRIOR WRITTEN PERMISSION OF THE COPYRIGHT OWNER. PUBLISHED IN GREAT BRITAIN
BY DORLING KINDERSLEY LIMITED.
DISTRIBUTED BY HOUGHTON MIFFLIN COMPANY, BOSTON.

LIBRARY OF CONGRESS CATALOGING-IN-PUBLICATION DATA

THE EYEWITNESS VISUAL DICTIONARY OF THE EARTH. — 1ST AMERICAN ED.
p. cm. — (THE EYEWITNESS VISUAL DICTIONARIES)
INCLUDES INDEX.

ISBN 1–56458–335–X
1. EARTH SCIENCES—TERMINOLOGY. 2. EARTH SCIENCES—PICTORIAL WORKS.
I. DORLING KINDERSLEY LIMITED. II. SERIES.

QE7.E94 1993   93-18571
550'.3—dc20   CIP

REPRODUCED BY COLOURSCAN, SINGAPORE
PRINTED AND BOUND IN ITALY BY ARNOLDO MONDADORI, VERONA

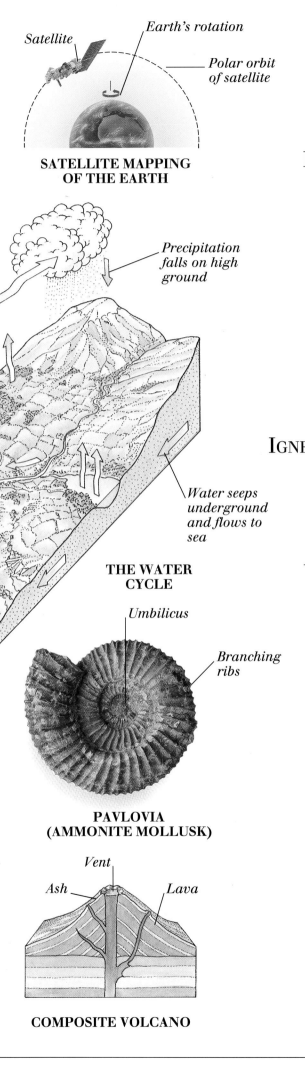

SATELLITE MAPPING OF THE EARTH

Satellite

Earth's rotation

Polar orbit of satellite

THE WATER CYCLE

Precipitation falls on high ground

Water seeps underground and flows to sea

PAVLOVIA (AMMONITE MOLLUSK)

Umbilicus

Branching ribs

COMPOSITE VOLCANO

Vent

Ash

Lava

Contents

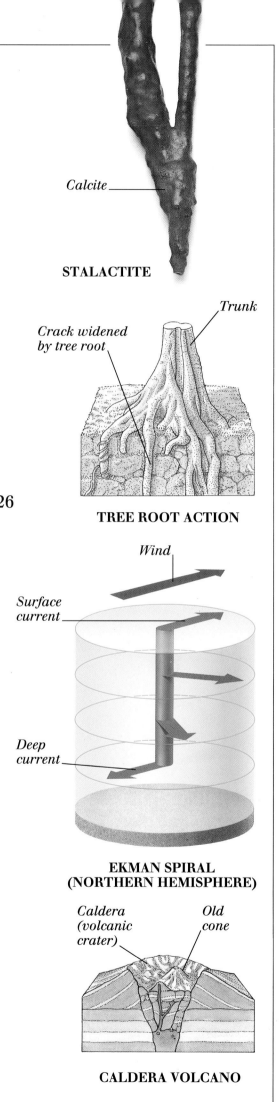

Calcite

STALACTITE

TREE ROOT ACTION

Trunk

Crack widened by tree root

EKMAN SPIRAL (NORTHERN HEMISPHERE)

Wind

Surface current

Deep current

CALDERA VOLCANO

Caldera (volcanic crater)

Old cone

Planet Earth

THE EARTH

The earth is one of the nine planets that orbit the Sun, which itself is just one of the approximately 100 billion stars in our galaxy—the Milky Way. Earth is the only planet that is known to support life. It is able to do so because it is the right distance from the Sun. If it were any nearer, conditions would be too hot for life; any farther away and it would be too cold. In addition, the Earth is the only planet known to have liquid water in large quantities. Its atmosphere helps to screen out some of the harmful radiation from the Sun, and also shields the planet from impacts by meteorites. The Earth consists of four main layers: an inner core, outer core, mantle, and crust. At the heart of the planet is the solid inner core, with a temperature of about 7,000°F. The heat from the inner core causes material in the molten outer core and mantle to circulate in convection currents. It is thought that these convection currents generate the Earth's magnetic field, which extends into space as the magnetosphere.

EARTH'S COORDINATE SYSTEM

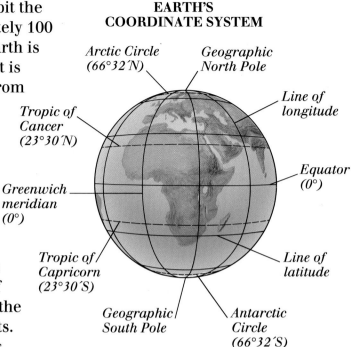

- Arctic Circle (66°32´N)
- Geographic North Pole
- Line of longitude
- Tropic of Cancer (23°30´N)
- Equator (0°)
- Greenwich meridian (0°)
- Line of latitude
- Tropic of Capricorn (23°30´S)
- Geographic South Pole
- Antarctic Circle (66°32´S)

EARTH'S PLACE IN THE SOLAR SYSTEM

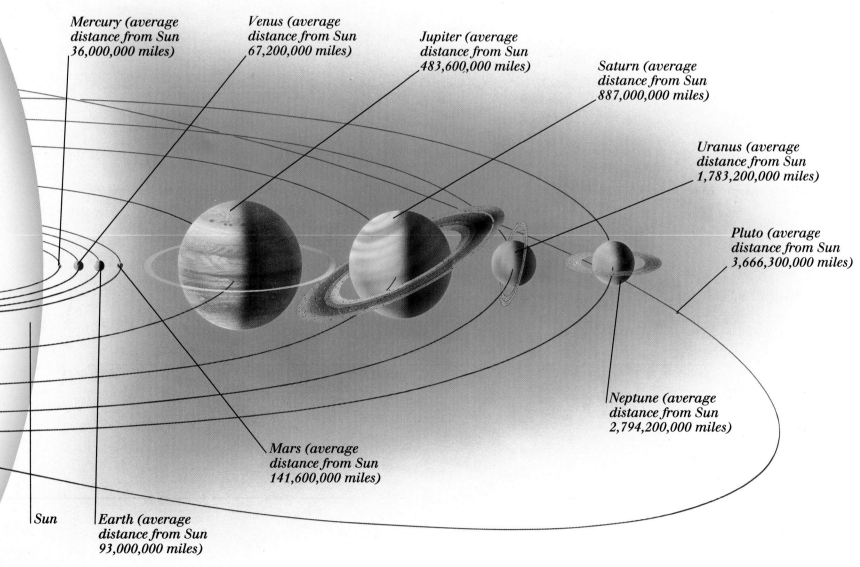

Mercury (average distance from Sun 36,000,000 miles)

Venus (average distance from Sun 67,200,000 miles)

Jupiter (average distance from Sun 483,600,000 miles)

Saturn (average distance from Sun 887,000,000 miles)

Uranus (average distance from Sun 1,783,200,000 miles)

Pluto (average distance from Sun 3,666,300,000 miles)

Neptune (average distance from Sun 2,794,200,000 miles)

Mars (average distance from Sun 141,600,000 miles)

Sun

Earth (average distance from Sun 93,000,000 miles)

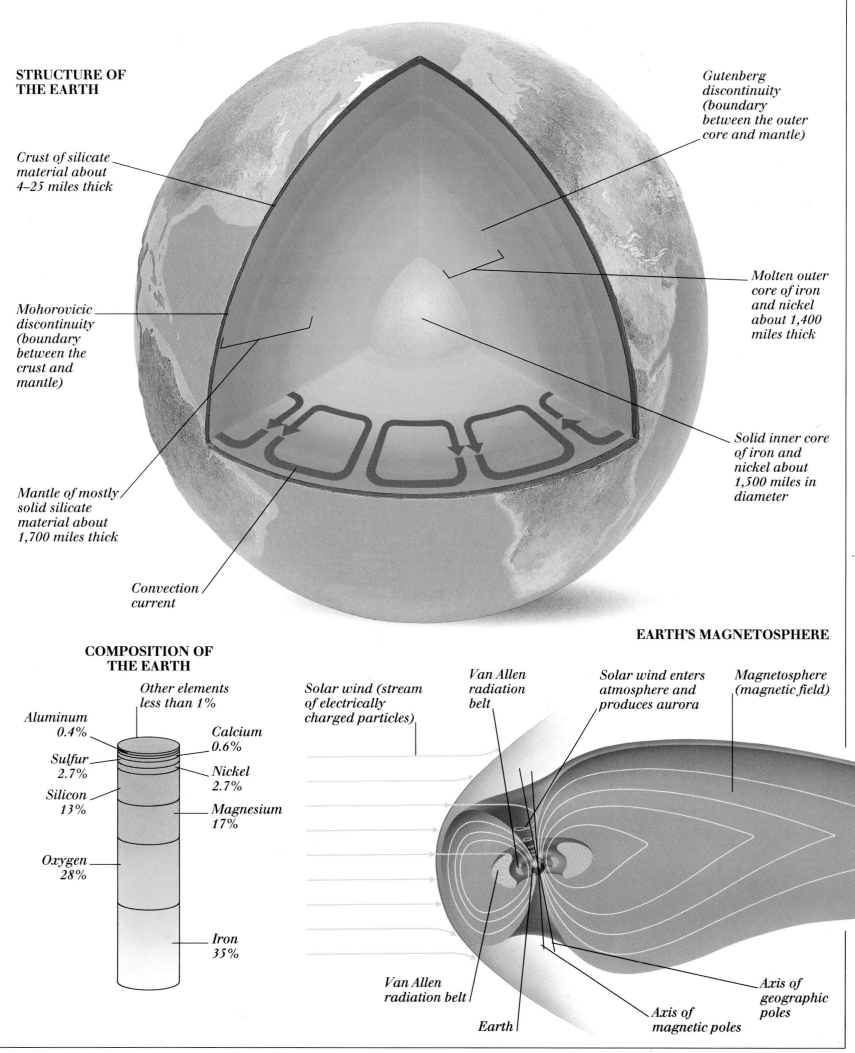

STRUCTURE OF THE EARTH

Crust of silicate material about 4–25 miles thick

Mohorovicic discontinuity (boundary between the crust and mantle)

Mantle of mostly solid silicate material about 1,700 miles thick

Convection current

Gutenberg discontinuity (boundary between the outer core and mantle)

Molten outer core of iron and nickel about 1,400 miles thick

Solid inner core of iron and nickel about 1,500 miles in diameter

COMPOSITION OF THE EARTH

Other elements less than 1%

Aluminum 0.4%

Sulfur 2.7%

Silicon 13%

Oxygen 28%

Calcium 0.6%

Nickel 2.7%

Magnesium 17%

Iron 35%

EARTH'S MAGNETOSPHERE

Solar wind (stream of electrically charged particles)

Van Allen radiation belt

Solar wind enters atmosphere and produces aurora

Magnetosphere (magnetic field)

Van Allen radiation belt

Earth

Axis of magnetic poles

Axis of geographic poles

Earth's physical features

MOST OF THE EARTH'S SURFACE (about 70 percent) is covered with water. The largest single body of water, the Pacific Ocean, alone covers about 30 percent of the surface. Most of the land is distributed as seven continents; these are (from largest to smallest) Asia, Africa, North America, South America, Antarctica, Europe, and Australasia. The physical features of the land are remarkably varied. Among the most notable are mountain ranges, rivers, and deserts. The largest mountain ranges—the Himalayas in Asia and the Andes in South America—extend for thousands of miles. The Himalayas include the world's highest mountain, Mount Everest (29,029 feet). The longest rivers are the River Nile in Africa (4,160 miles) and the Amazon River in South America (4,000 miles). Deserts cover about 20 percent of the total land area. The largest is the Sahara, which covers nearly a third of Africa. The Earth's surface features can be represented in various ways. Only a globe can correctly represent areas, shapes, sizes, and directions, because there is always distortion when a spherical surface like the Earth's is projected onto the flat surface of a map. Each map projection is therefore a compromise: some aspects of global features are shown accurately by allowing others to be distorted. Even satellite mapping does not produce completely accurate maps, although they can show physical features with great clarity.

EXAMPLES OF MAP PROJECTIONS

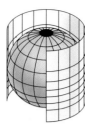

CYLINDRICAL PROJECTION

CYLINDRICAL-PROJECTION MAP

SATELLITE MAPPING OF THE EARTH

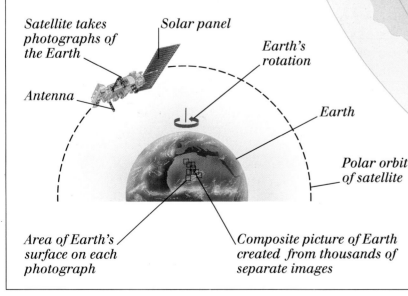

Satellite takes photographs of the Earth

Solar panel

Earth's rotation

Antenna

Earth

Polar orbit of satellite

Area of Earth's surface on each photograph

Composite picture of Earth created from thousands of separate images

180°   160°   120°   80°

Great Slave Lake   Great Bear Lake   Lake Superior

Mackenzie-Peace River

Greenland

Bering Sea

Hudson Bay

Baffin Island

Rocky Mountains

NORTH AMERICA

Mississippi-Missouri River

Lake Huron
Lake Ontario
Lake Erie
Lake Michigan

Sonoran Desert

Sierra Madre

Appalachian Mountains

Gulf of Mexico

ATLANTIC OCEAN

Chihuahuan Desert

Caribbean Sea

Guiana Highlands

Amazon River

Brazilian Highlan

PACIFIC OCEAN

Andes

Atacama Desert

Gran Chaco

Mato Grosso

Parana River

Pampas

Patagonia

120°   80°

180°   160°

WEST OF GREENWICH MERIDIAN

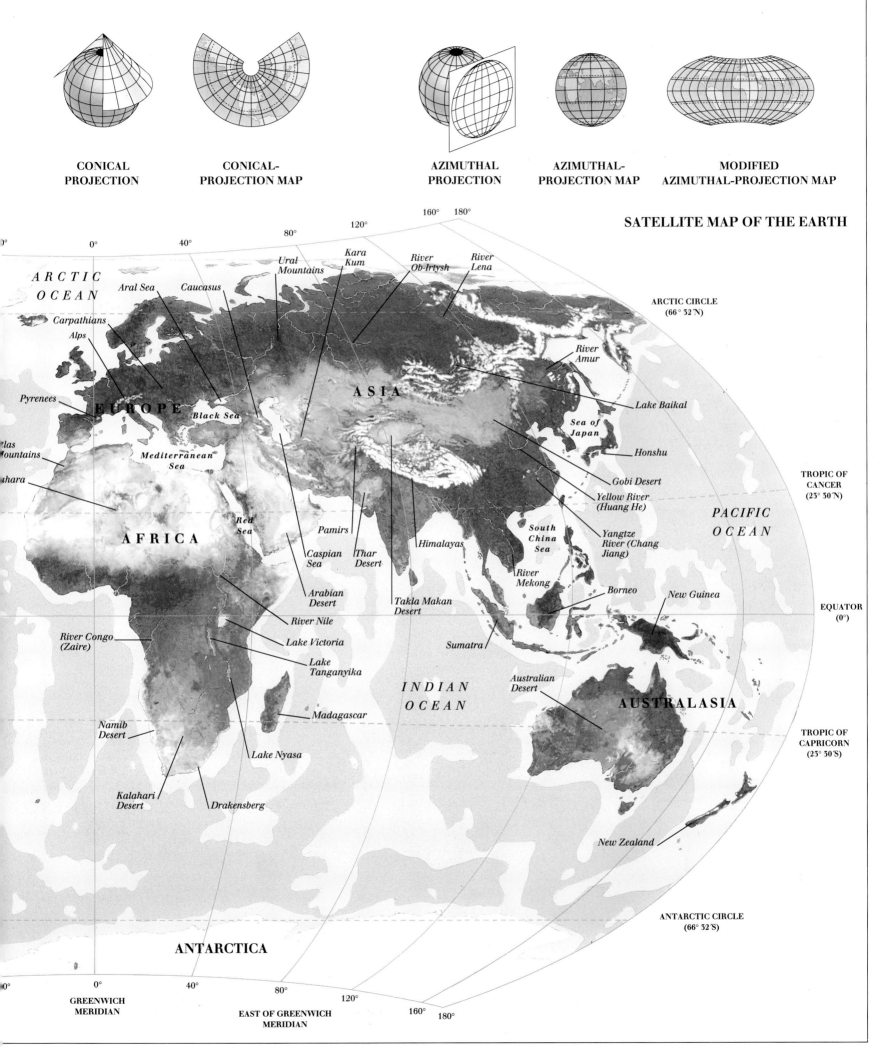

CONICAL
PROJECTION

CONICAL-
PROJECTION MAP

AZIMUTHAL
PROJECTION

AZIMUTHAL-
PROJECTION MAP

MODIFIED
AZIMUTHAL-PROJECTION MAP

SATELLITE MAP OF THE EARTH

160° 180°

120°

80°

0°

40°

*ARCTIC
OCEAN*

ARCTIC CIRCLE
(66° 52′N)

Carpathians

Aral Sea

Caucasus

*Ural
Mountains*

*Kara
Kum*

*River
Ob-Irtysh*

*River
Lena*

Alps

*River
Amur*

Pyrenees

E U R O P E

Black Sea

A S I A

Lake Baikal

*Sea of
Japan*

*las
Mountains*

*Mediterranean
Sea*

Honshu

Gobi Desert

TROPIC OF
CANCER
(23° 30′N)

ahara

*Yellow River
(Huang He)*

*PACIFIC
OCEAN*

*Red
Sea*

A F R I C A

Pamirs

Himalayas

*South
China
Sea*

*Yangtze
River (Chang
Jiang)*

*Caspian
Sea*

*Thar
Desert*

*River
Mekong*

*Arabian
Desert*

*Takla Makan
Desert*

Borneo

New Guinea

EQUATOR
(0°)

River Nile

*River Congo
(Zaire)*

Lake Victoria

Sumatra

*Lake
Tanganyika*

*INDIAN
OCEAN*

*Australian
Desert*

AUSTRALASIA

Madagascar

*Namib
Desert*

Lake Nyasa

TROPIC OF
CAPRICORN
(23° 30′S)

*Kalahari
Desert*

Drakensberg

New Zealand

ANTARCTIC CIRCLE
(66° 52′S)

ANTARCTICA

0°

0°

40°

80°

120°

160° 180°

GREENWICH
MERIDIAN

EAST OF GREENWICH
MERIDIAN

9

Geological time

THE EARTH FORMED FROM A CLOUD OF DUST and gas drifting through space about 4,600 million years ago. Dense minerals sank to the center while lighter ones formed a thin rocky crust. However, the first known life forms—bacteria and blue-green algae—did not appear until about 3,500 million years ago, and it was only about 570 million years ago that more complex plants and animals began to develop. Since then, thousands of animal and plant species have evolved. Some have thrived: others, such as the dinosaurs, have died out. Like the species that inhabit it, the Earth itself is continually changing. The continents neared their present locations about 50 million years ago, but are still drifting slowly over the planet's surface, and mountain ranges such as the Himalayas—which began to form 40 million years ago—are continually being built up and worn away. Climate is also subject to change: the Earth has undergone a series of ice ages and glacial periods (the most recent glacial period occurred about 20,000 years ago) interspersed with warmer periods.

Small mammals appeared (e.g., Crusafontia)

Dinosaurs became extinct

Global mountain building occurred

Multicellular soft-bodied animals appeared (e.g., worms and jellyfish)

Shelled invertebrates appeared (e.g., trilobites)

Marine plants flourished

Land plants appeared (e.g., Cooksonia)

Unicellular organisms appeared (e.g., blue-green algae)

CRETACEOU

ORDOVICIAN   CAMBRIAN   PRECAMBRIAN TIME

SILURIAN   DEVONIAN

Earth formed

Coral reefs appeared

Vertebrates appeared (e.g., Hemicyclaspis)

More complex types of algae appeared

Amphibians appeared (e.g., Ichthyostega)

GEOLOGICAL TIMESCALE

MILLIONS OF YEARS AGO (MYA)

4,600		550		505		438		408		360		320		286

PRECAMBRIAN TIME	CAMBRIAN	ORDOVICIAN	SILURIAN	DEVONIAN	MISSISSIPPIAN (NORTH AMERICA)	PENNSYLVANIAN (NORTH AMERICA)
					CARBONIFEROUS	
	PALEOZOIC					

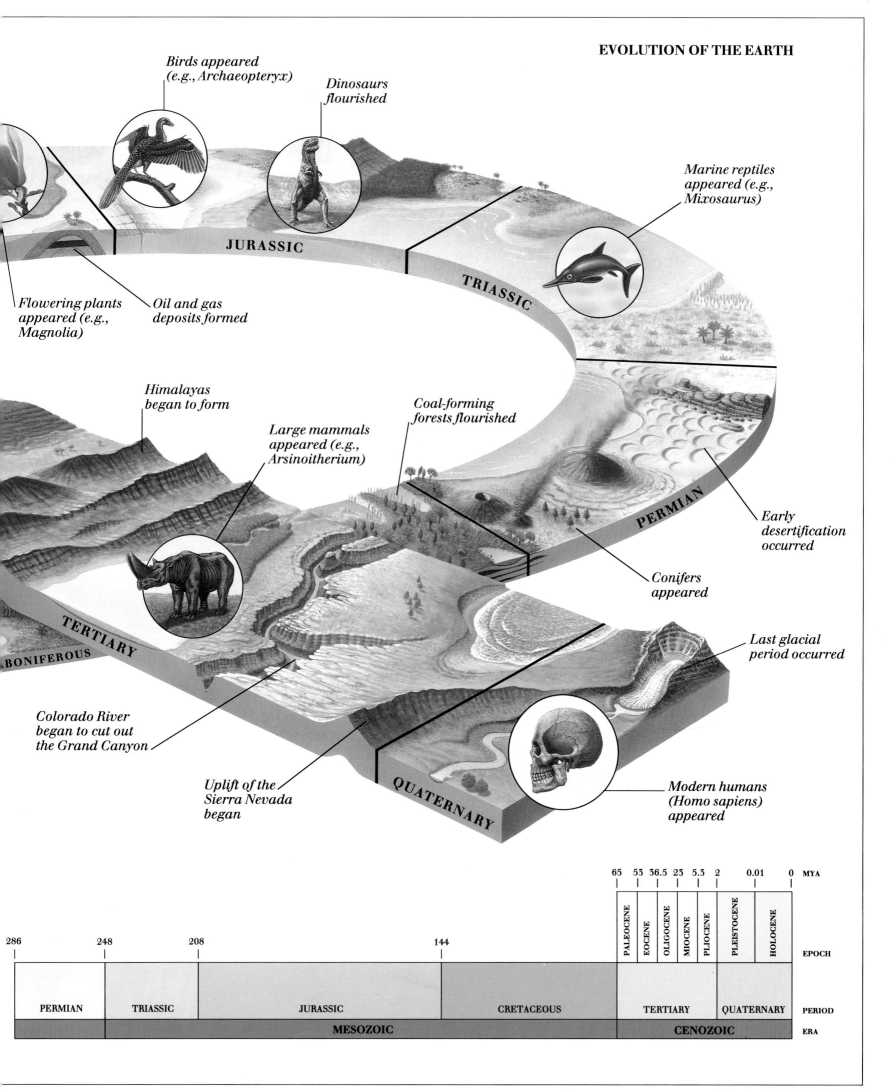

EVOLUTION OF THE EARTH

Birds appeared (e.g., Archaeopteryx)

Dinosaurs flourished

Marine reptiles appeared (e.g., Mixosaurus)

JURASSIC

TRIASSIC

Flowering plants appeared (e.g., Magnolia)

Oil and gas deposits formed

Himalayas began to form

Large mammals appeared (e.g., Arsinoitherium)

Coal-forming forests flourished

PERMIAN

Early desertification occurred

Conifers appeared

TERTIARY

BONIFEROUS

Last glacial period occurred

Colorado River began to cut out the Grand Canyon

Uplift of the Sierra Nevada began

QUATERNARY

Modern humans (Homo sapiens) appeared

65	53	36.5	23	5.3	2	0.01	0	MYA

PALEOCENE	EOCENE	OLIGOCENE	MIOCENE	PLIOCENE	PLEISTOCENE	HOLOCENE	EPOCH

286		248		208				144							

PERMIAN	TRIASSIC	JURASSIC	CRETACEOUS	TERTIARY	QUATERNARY	PERIOD
	MESOZOIC				CENOZOIC	ERA

Earth's crust

THE EARTH'S CRUST IS THE SOLID OUTER shell of the Earth. It includes continental crust (about 25 miles thick) and oceanic crust (about four miles thick). The crust and the topmost layer of the mantle form the lithosphere. The lithosphere consists of semirigid plates that move relative to each other on the underlying asthenosphere (a partly molten layer of the mantle). This process is known as plate tectonics. Where two plates move apart there are rifts in the crust. In midocean, this movement results in seafloor spreading and the formation of ocean ridges; on continents, crustal spreading can form rift valleys. When plates move toward each other, one may be subducted beneath (forced under) the other. In midocean, this process results in ocean trenches, seismic activity, and arcs of volcanic islands. Mountains may be uplifted where oceanic crust is subducted beneath continental crust, or where continents collide (see pp. 16-17). Plates may also slide past each other—along the San Andreas fault, for example. Plate tectonics helps explain continental drift—the theory that the world's continents moved together about 175 million years ago to form a single landmass called Pangaea, which has subsequently split up.

ELEMENTS IN THE EARTH'S CRUST

Other elements 2%
Potassium 2.6%
Sodium 2.8%
Iron 5%
Magnesium 2%
Calcium 3.6%
Aluminum 8%
Silicon 28%
Oxygen 46%

FEATURES OF PLATE MOVEMENTS

Ridge where magma is rising to form new oceanic crust

Region of seafloor spreading

Ocean trench formed where oceanic crust is forced under continental crust

Subduction zone

Rift formed where two plates are moving apart

Magma (molten rock) erupts at rift

Magma rises to form a hot spot

Volcano develops over hot spot and builds up to form an island

Volcanic island that originally formed over hot spot

Oceanic crust melts

Magma rises to form a volcano

MAJOR PLATES OF THE EARTH'S CRUST

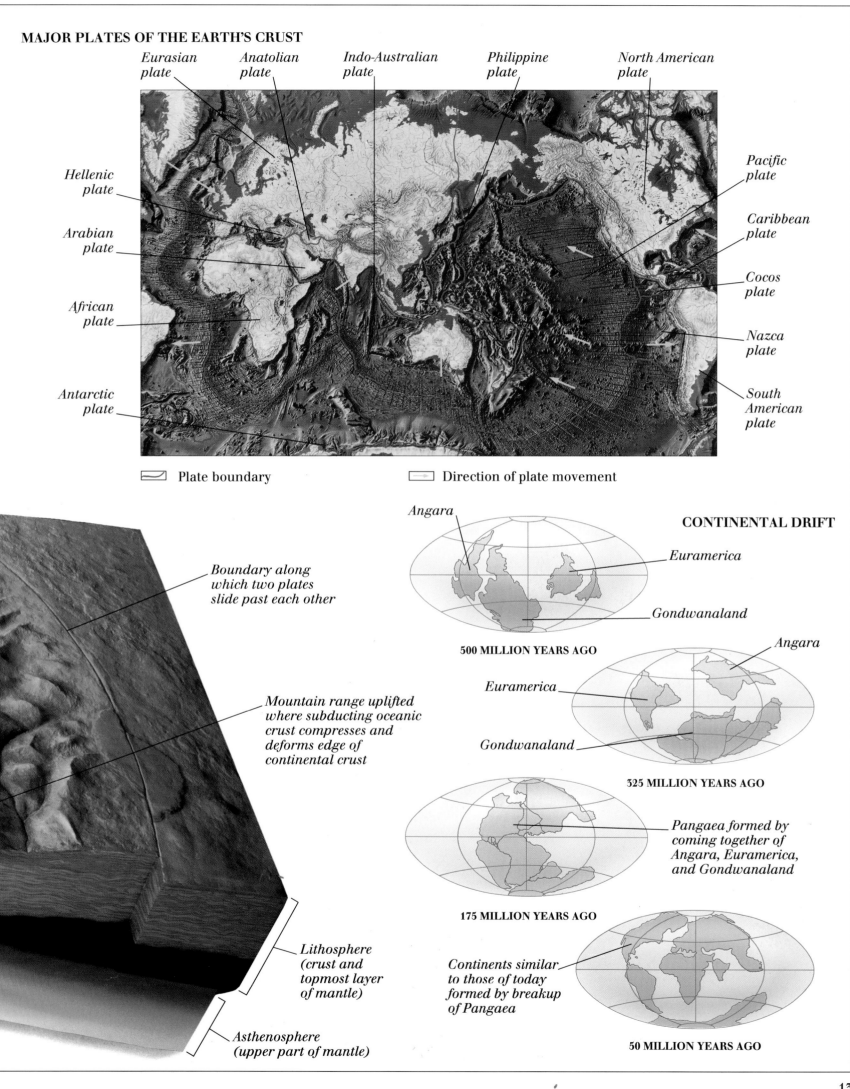

Eurasian plate

Anatolian plate

Indo-Australian plate

Philippine plate

North American plate

Hellenic plate

Arabian plate

African plate

Antarctic plate

Pacific plate

Caribbean plate

Cocos plate

Nazca plate

South American plate

Plate boundary

Direction of plate movement

Boundary along which two plates slide past each other

Mountain range uplifted where subducting oceanic crust compresses and deforms edge of continental crust

Lithosphere (crust and topmost layer of mantle)

Asthenosphere (upper part of mantle)

CONTINENTAL DRIFT

Angara

Euramerica

Gondwanaland

500 MILLION YEARS AGO

Euramerica

Angara

Gondwanaland

325 MILLION YEARS AGO

Pangaea formed by coming together of Angara, Euramerica, and Gondwanaland

175 MILLION YEARS AGO

Continents similar to those of today formed by breakup of Pangaea

50 MILLION YEARS AGO

13

Faults and folds

THE CONTINUOUS MOVEMENT of the Earth's crustal plates (see pp. 12-13) can squeeze, stretch, or break rock strata, deforming them and producing faults and folds. A fault is a fracture in a rock along which there is movement of one side relative to the other. The movement can be vertical, horizontal, or oblique (vertical and horizontal). Faults develop when rocks are subjected to compression or tension. Faults tend to occur in hard, rigid rocks, which are more likely to break rather than bend. The smallest faults occur in single mineral crystals and are microscopically small, while the largest—the Great Rift Valley in Africa—is more than 6,000 miles long. Movement along faults is a common cause of earthquakes. A fold is a bend in a rock layer caused by compression. Folds occur in elastic rocks, which tend to bend rather than break. The two main types of folds are anticlines (upfolds) and synclines (downfolds). Folds vary in size from a few millimeters long to folded mountain ranges hundreds of miles long. In addition to faults and folds, other features associated with rock deformations include boudins, mullions, and *en échelon* fractures.

STRUCTURE OF A FOLD

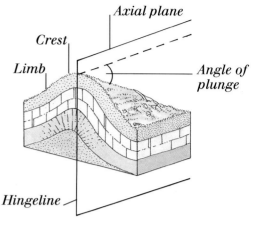

Axial plane

Crest

Limb

Angle of plunge

Hingeline

STRUCTURE OF A FAULT

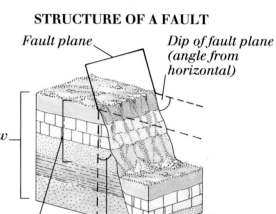

Fault plane

Dip of fault plane (angle from horizontal)

Upthrow

Throw (vertical displacement of fault)

Downthrow

Hade of fault plane (angle from vertical)

STRUCTURE OF A SLOPE

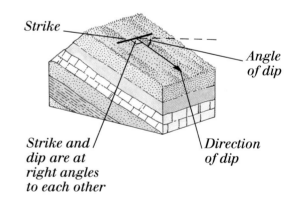

Strike

Angle of dip

Strike and dip are at right angles to each other

Direction of dip

FOLDED ROCK

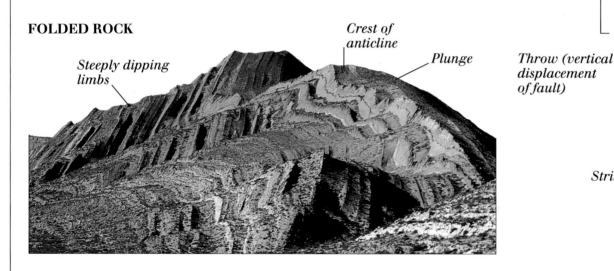

Steeply dipping limbs

Crest of anticline

Plunge

SECTION THROUGH FOLDED ROCK STRATA THAT HAVE BEEN ERODED

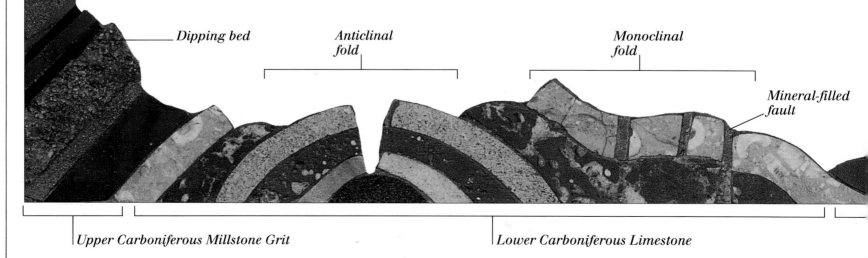

Dipping bed

Anticlinal fold

Monoclinal fold

Mineral-filled fault

Upper Carboniferous Millstone Grit

Lower Carboniferous Limestone

EXAMPLES OF FOLDS

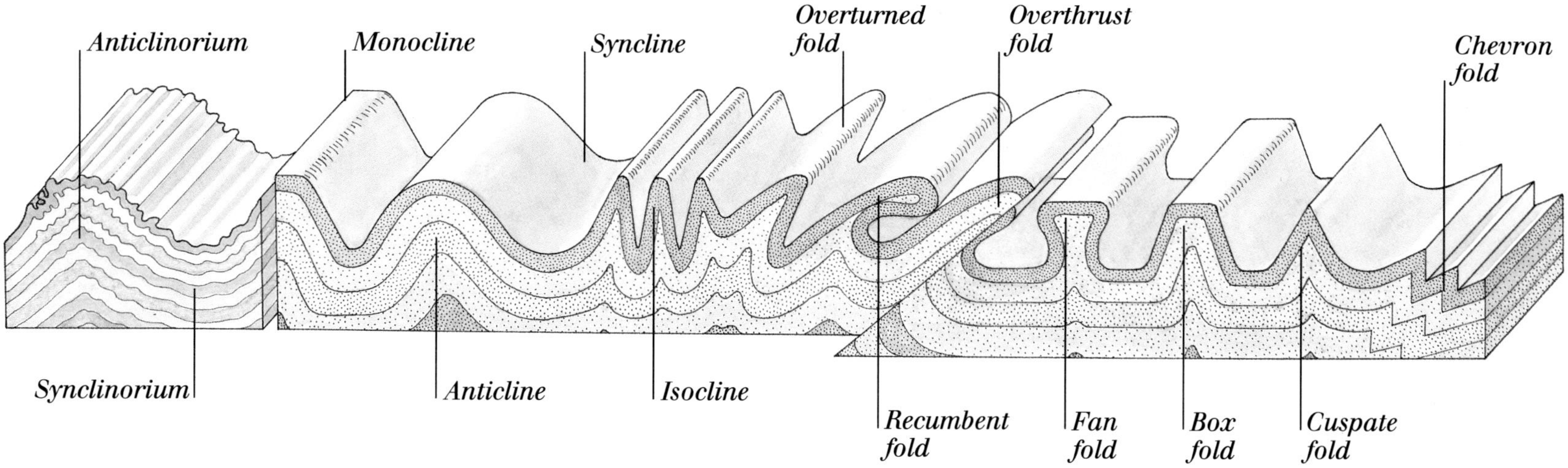

Anticlinorium

Monocline

Syncline

Overturned fold

Overthrust fold

Chevron fold

Synclinorium

Anticline

Isocline

Recumbent fold

Fan fold

Box fold

Cuspate fold

EXAMPLES OF FAULTS

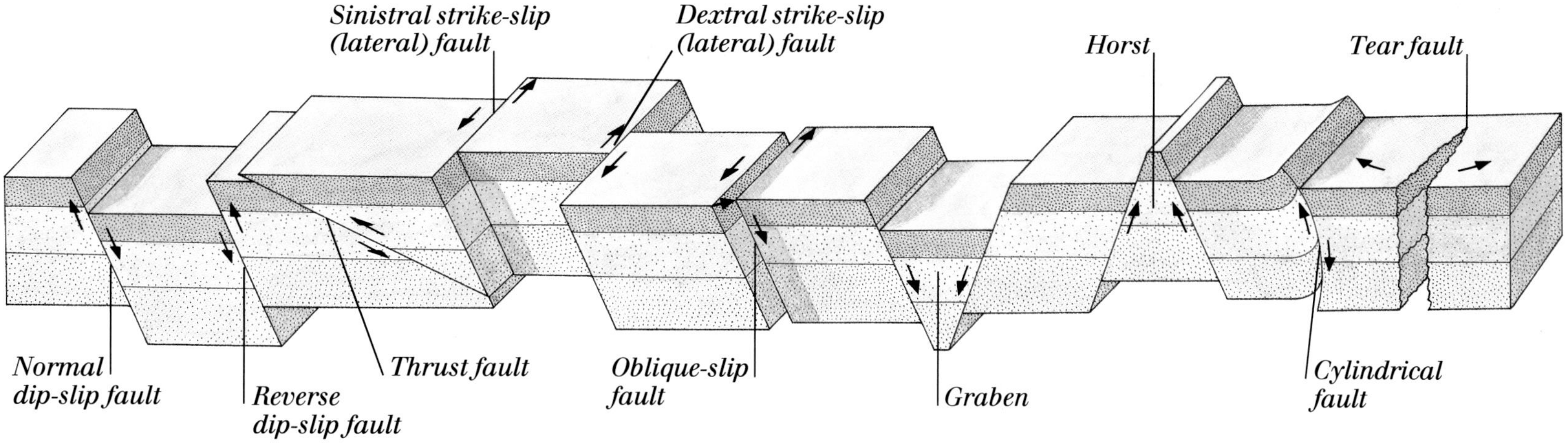

Sinistral strike-slip (lateral) fault

Dextral strike-slip (lateral) fault

Horst

Tear fault

Normal dip-slip fault

Reverse dip-slip fault

Thrust fault

Oblique-slip fault

Graben

Cylindrical fault

SMALL-SCALE ROCK DEFORMATIONS

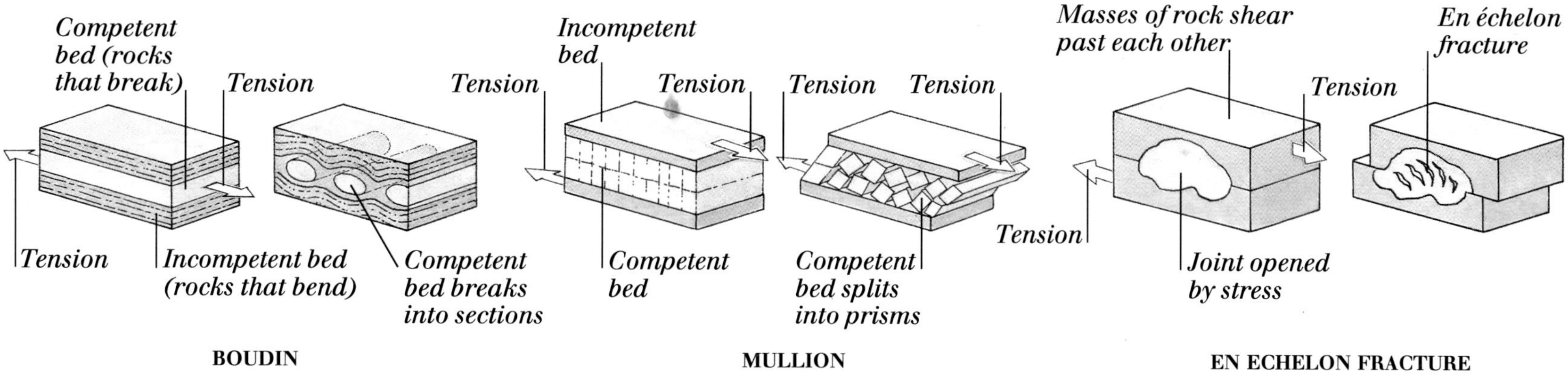

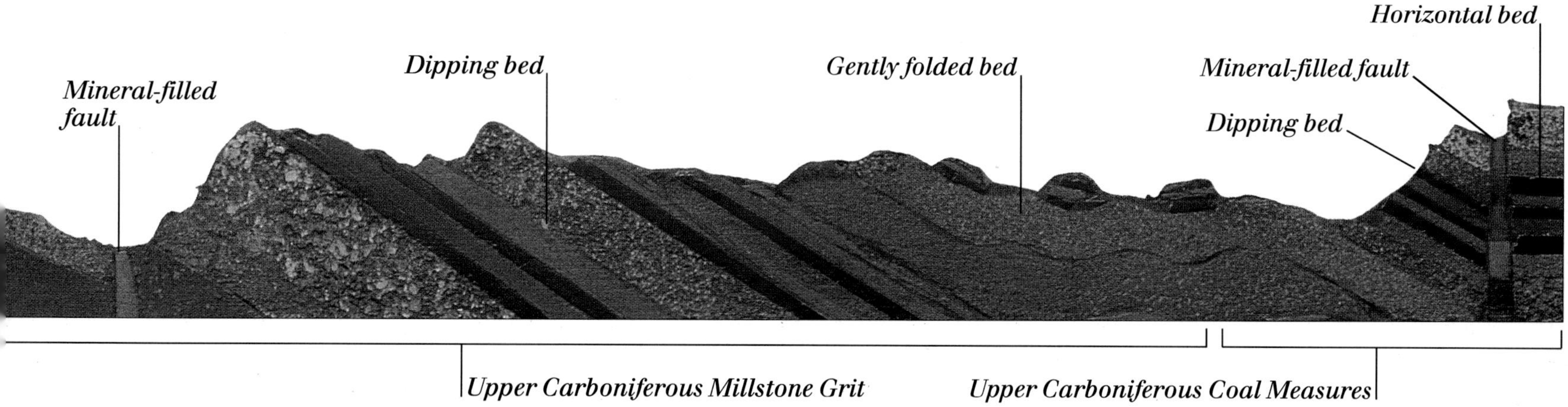

Competent bed (rocks that break)

Tension

Incompetent bed

Tension

Tension

Tension

Masses of rock shear past each other

En échelon fracture

Tension

Tension

Incompetent bed (rocks that bend)

Competent bed breaks into sections

Competent bed

Competent bed splits into prisms

Tension

Joint opened by stress

BOUDIN

MULLION

EN ECHELON FRACTURE

Horizontal bed

Dipping bed

Gently folded bed

Mineral-filled fault

Mineral-filled fault

Dipping bed

Upper Carboniferous Millstone Grit

Upper Carboniferous Coal Measures

Mountain building

THE PROCESSES INVOLVED in mountain building—termed orogenesis—occur as a result of the movement of the Earth's crustal plates (see pp. 12-13). There are three main types of mountains: volcanic mountains, fold mountains, and block mountains. Most volcanic mountains are formed along plate boundaries where plates come together or move apart (see pp. 18-19) and lava and other debris is ejected on to the Earth's surface. The lava and debris may build up to form a dome around the vent of a volcano. Fold mountains are

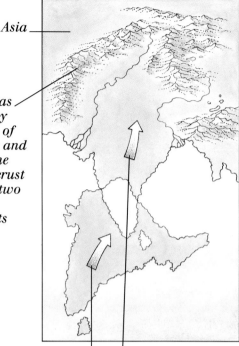

Asia

Himalayas formed by buckling of sediment and part of the oceanic crust between two colliding continents

India moves north

India collides with Asia about 40 million years ago

formed where plates push together and cause the rock to buckle upward. Where oceanic crust meets less dense continental crust, the oceanic crust is forced under the continental crust. The continental crust is buckled by the impact, and folded mountain ranges, such as the Appalachian Mountains in North America, are formed. Fold mountains are also formed where two areas of continental crust meet. The Himalayas, for example, began to form

BHAGIRATHI PARBAT, HIMALAYAS

when India collided with Asia, buckling the sediments and parts of the oceanic crust between them. Block mountains are formed when a block of land is uplifted between two faults as a result of compression or tension in the Earth's crust (see pp. 14-15). Often, the movement along faults takes place gradually over millions of years. However, two plates may slide past each other suddenly along a faultline—the San Andreas fault, for example—causing earthquakes.

EXAMPLES OF MOUNTAINS

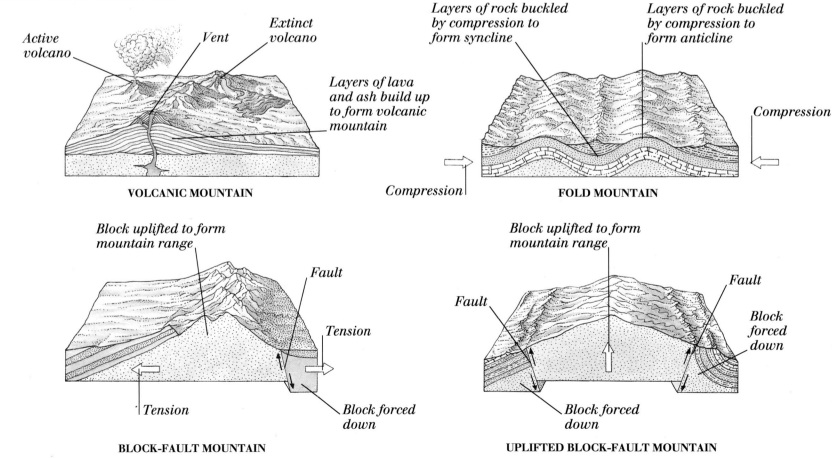

Active volcano

Vent

Extinct volcano

Layers of lava and ash build up to form volcanic mountain

VOLCANIC MOUNTAIN

Layers of rock buckled by compression to form syncline

Layers of rock buckled by compression to form anticline

Compression

Compression

FOLD MOUNTAIN

Block uplifted to form mountain range

Fault

Tension

Tension

Block forced down

BLOCK-FAULT MOUNTAIN

Block uplifted to form mountain range

Fault

Fault

Block forced down

Block forced down

UPLIFTED BLOCK-FAULT MOUNTAIN

STAGES IN THE FORMATION OF THE HIMALAYAS

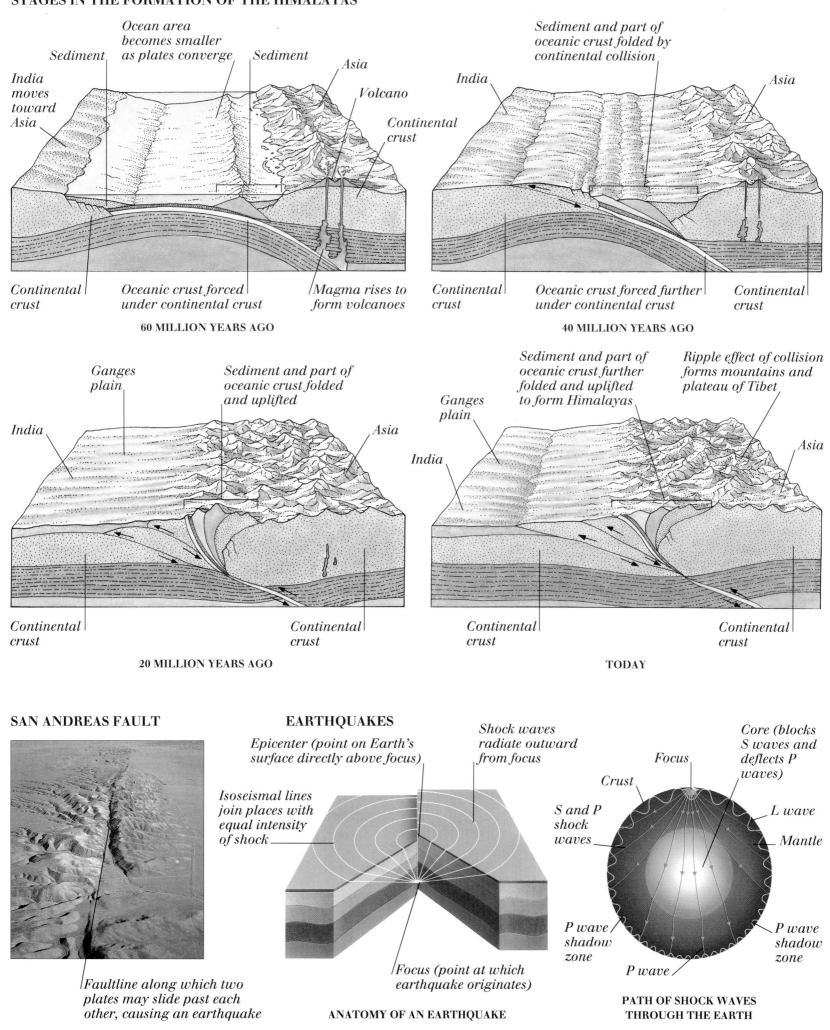

Ocean area becomes smaller as plates converge

Sediment

India moves toward Asia

Sediment

Asia

Volcano

Continental crust

Continental crust

Oceanic crust forced under continental crust

Magma rises to form volcanoes

60 MILLION YEARS AGO

Sediment and part of oceanic crust folded by continental collision

India

Asia

Continental crust

Oceanic crust forced further under continental crust

Continental crust

40 MILLION YEARS AGO

Ganges plain

Sediment and part of oceanic crust folded and uplifted

India

Asia

Continental crust

Continental crust

20 MILLION YEARS AGO

Sediment and part of oceanic crust further folded and uplifted to form Himalayas

Ripple effect of collision forms mountains and plateau of Tibet

Ganges plain

India

Asia

Continental crust

Continental crust

TODAY

SAN ANDREAS FAULT

Faultline along which two plates may slide past each other, causing an earthquake

EARTHQUAKES

Epicenter (point on Earth's surface directly above focus)

Shock waves radiate outward from focus

Isoseismal lines join places with equal intensity of shock

Focus (point at which earthquake originates)

ANATOMY OF AN EARTHQUAKE

Core (blocks S waves and deflects P waves)

Focus

Crust

S and P shock waves

L wave

Mantle

P wave shadow zone

P wave

P wave shadow zone

PATH OF SHOCK WAVES THROUGH THE EARTH

Volcanoes

VOLCANOES ARE VENTS OR FISSURES IN THE EARTH'S crust through which magma (molten rock that originates from deep beneath the crust) is forced onto the surface as lava. They occur most commonly along the boundaries of crustal plates; most volcanoes lie in a belt called the "Ring of Fire," which runs along the edge of the Pacific Ocean. Volcanoes can be classified according to the violence and frequency of their eruptions.

Nonexplosive volcanic eruptions generally occur where crustal plates pull apart. These eruptions produce runny basaltic lava that spreads quickly over a wide area to form relatively flat cones. The most violent eruptions take place where plates collide. Such eruptions produce thick rhyolitic lava and may also blast out clouds of dust and pyroclasts (lava fragments). The lava does not flow far before cooling and therefore builds up steep-sided, conical volcanoes. Some volcanoes produce lava and ash eruptions, which build up composite volcanic cones. Volcanoes that erupt frequently are described as active, those that erupt rarely are termed dormant, and those that have stopped erupting altogether are termed extinct. Besides the volcanoes themselves, other features associated with volcanic regions include geysers, hot mineral springs, solfataras, fumaroles, and bubbling mud pools.

Folded, rope-like surface

PAHOEHOE (ROPY LAVA)

HORU GEYSER, NEW ZEALAND

VOLCANO TYPES

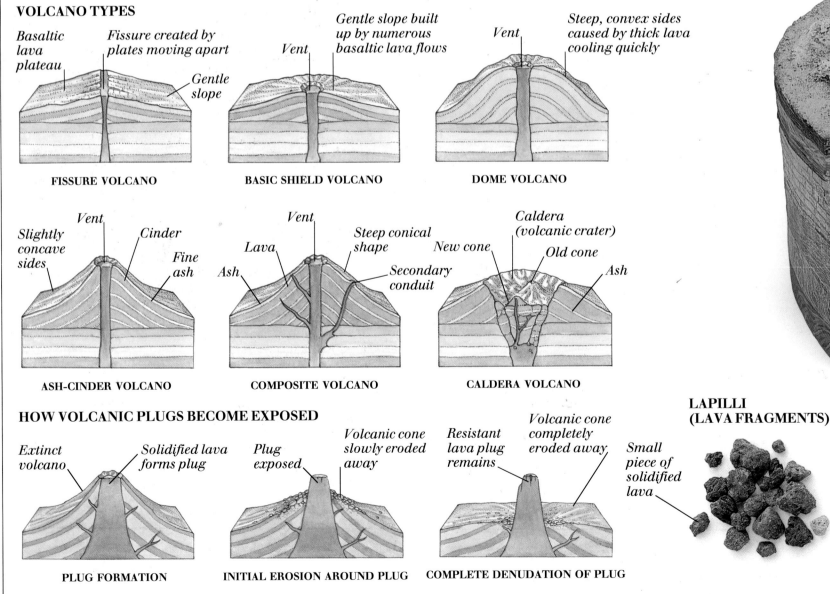

Basaltic lava plateau

Fissure created by plates moving apart

Gentle slope

FISSURE VOLCANO

Gentle slope built up by numerous basaltic lava flows

Vent

BASIC SHIELD VOLCANO

Vent

Steep, convex sides caused by thick lava cooling quickly

DOME VOLCANO

Vent

Slightly concave sides

Cinder

Fine ash

ASH-CINDER VOLCANO

Vent

Lava

Ash

Steep conical shape

Secondary conduit

COMPOSITE VOLCANO

Caldera (volcanic crater)

New cone

Old cone

Ash

CALDERA VOLCANO

HOW VOLCANIC PLUGS BECOME EXPOSED

Extinct volcano

Solidified lava forms plug

PLUG FORMATION

Plug exposed

Volcanic cone slowly eroded away

INITIAL EROSION AROUND PLUG

Resistant lava plug remains

Volcanic cone completely eroded away

COMPLETE DENUDATION OF PLUG

LAPILLI (LAVA FRAGMENTS)

Small piece of solidified lava

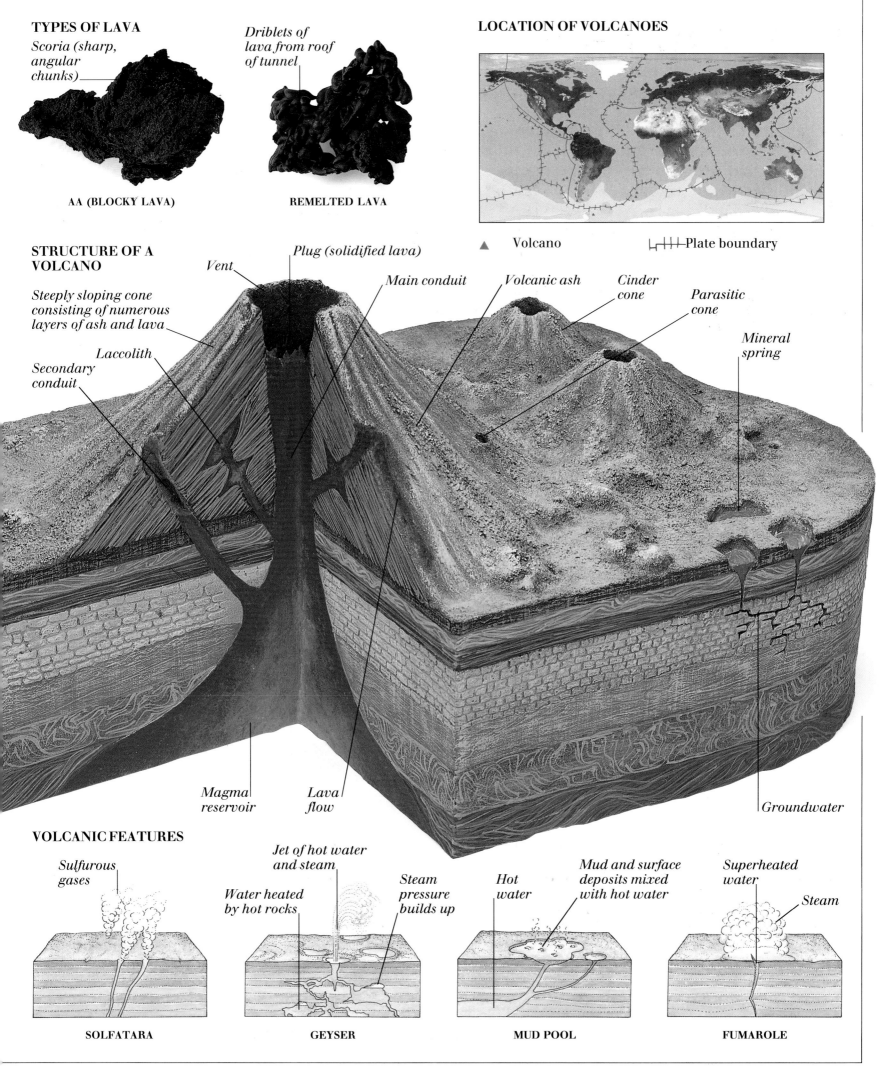

TYPES OF LAVA

Scoria (sharp, angular chunks)

Driblets of lava from roof of tunnel

AA (BLOCKY LAVA)

REMELTED LAVA

LOCATION OF VOLCANOES

▲ Volcano   Plate boundary

STRUCTURE OF A VOLCANO

Steeply sloping cone consisting of numerous layers of ash and lava

Vent

Plug (solidified lava)

Main conduit

Volcanic ash

Cinder cone

Parasitic cone

Mineral spring

Laccolith

Secondary conduit

Magma reservoir

Lava flow

Groundwater

VOLCANIC FEATURES

Sulfurous gases

Jet of hot water and steam

Water heated by hot rocks

Steam pressure builds up

Hot water

Mud and surface deposits mixed with hot water

Superheated water

Steam

SOLFATARA

GEYSER

MUD POOL

FUMAROLE

The rock cycle

THE ROCK CYCLE IS A CONTINUOUS PROCESS through which old rocks are transformed into new ones. Rocks can be divided into three main groups: igneous, sedimentary, and metamorphic. Igneous rocks are formed when magma (molten rock) from the Earth's interior cools and solidifies (see pp. 26-27). Sedimentary rocks are formed when sediment (rock particles, for example) becomes compressed and cemented together in a process known as lithification (see pp. 28-29). Metamorphic rocks are formed when igneous, sedimentary, or other metamorphic rocks are changed by heat or pressure (see pp. 26-27). Rocks are added to the Earth's surface by crustal movements and volcanic activity. Once exposed on the surface, the rocks are broken down into rock particles by weathering (see pp. 34-35). The particles are then transported by glaciers, rivers, and wind and are deposited as sediment in lakes, deltas, deserts, and on the ocean floor. Some of this sediment undergoes lithification and forms sedimentary rock. This rock may be thrust back to the surface by crustal movements or forced deeper into the Earth's interior, where heat and pressure transform it into metamorphic rock. The metamorphic rock in turn may be pushed up to the surface or may be melted to form magma. Eventually, the magma cools and solidifies—below or on the surface—forming igneous rock. When the sedimentary, igneous, and metamorphic rocks are exposed once more on the Earth's surface, the cycle begins again.

HEXAGONAL BASALT
COLUMNS, ICELAND

THE ROCK CYCLE

Igneous rock

Weathering, transport, and deposition

Sediment

Cooling and solidification (crystallization)

Heat and pressure (metamorphism)

Weathering, transport, and deposition

Weathering, transport, and deposition

Compression and cementation (lithification)

Magma

Melting

Heat and pressure (metamorphism)

Metamorphic rock

Sedimentary rock

STAGES IN THE ROCK CYCLE

Magma extruded as lava, which solidifies to form igneous rock

Lava flow

Vent

Main conduit

Secondary conduit

Lava

Ash

Rock surrounding magma changed by heat to form metamorphic rock

Intense heat of rising magma melts some of the surrounding rock

Sedimentary rock crushed and folded to form metamorphic rock

20

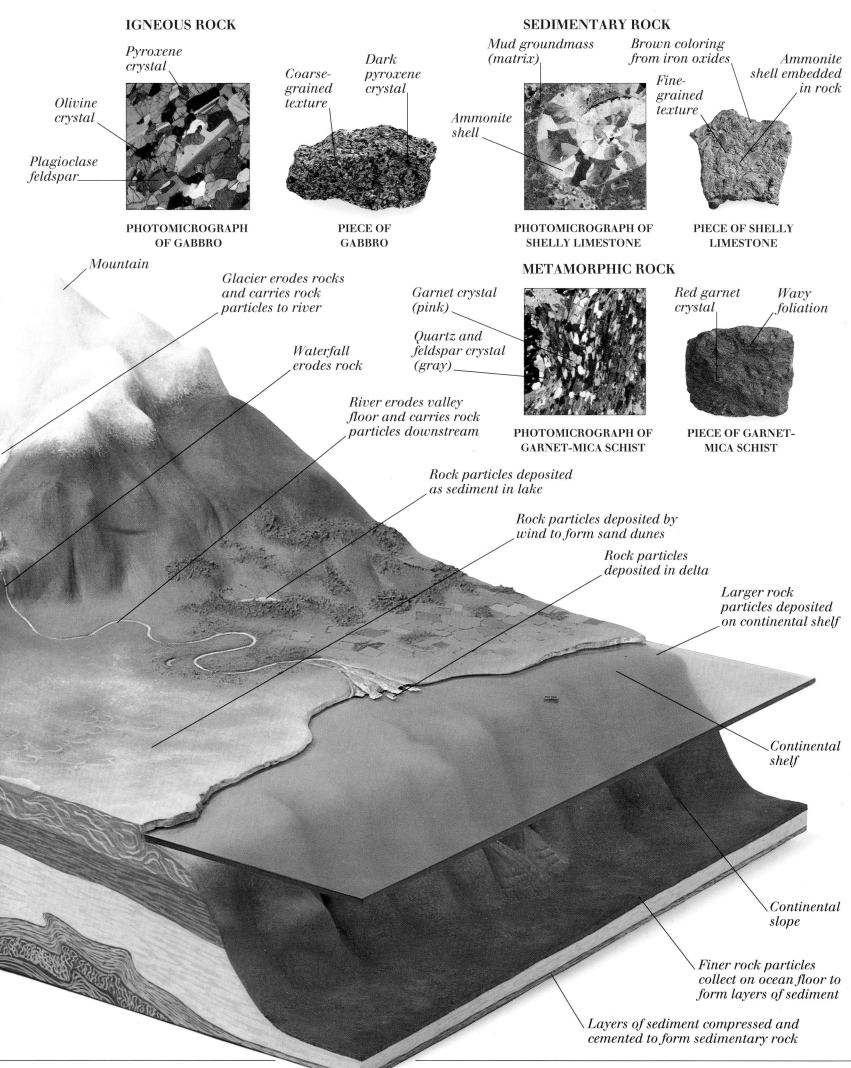

IGNEOUS ROCK

Pyroxene crystal

Olivine crystal

Plagioclase feldspar

Coarse-grained texture

Dark pyroxene crystal

PHOTOMICROGRAPH OF GABBRO

PIECE OF GABBRO

SEDIMENTARY ROCK

Mud groundmass (matrix)

Brown coloring from iron oxides

Fine-grained texture

Ammonite shell embedded in rock

Ammonite shell

PHOTOMICROGRAPH OF SHELLY LIMESTONE

PIECE OF SHELLY LIMESTONE

METAMORPHIC ROCK

Garnet crystal (pink)

Quartz and feldspar crystal (gray)

Red garnet crystal

Wavy foliation

PHOTOMICROGRAPH OF GARNET-MICA SCHIST

PIECE OF GARNET-MICA SCHIST

Mountain

Glacier erodes rocks and carries rock particles to river

Waterfall erodes rock

River erodes valley floor and carries rock particles downstream

Rock particles deposited as sediment in lake

Rock particles deposited by wind to form sand dunes

Rock particles deposited in delta

Larger rock particles deposited on continental shelf

Continental shelf

Continental slope

Finer rock particles collect on ocean floor to form layers of sediment

Layers of sediment compressed and cemented to form sedimentary rock

Minerals

A MINERAL IS A NATURALLY OCCURRING SUBSTANCE that has a characteristic chemical composition and specific physical properties, such as habit and streak (see pp. 24-25). A rock, by comparison, is an aggregate of minerals and need not have a specific chemical composition. Minerals are made up of elements (substances that cannot be broken down chemically into simpler substances), each of which can be represented by a chemical symbol (see p. 58). Minerals can be divided into two main groups: native elements and compounds. Native elements are made up of a pure element. Examples include gold (chemical symbol Au), silver (Ag), copper (Cu), and carbon (C); carbon occurs as a native element in two forms, diamond and graphite. Compounds are combinations of two or more elements. For example, sulfides are compounds of sulfur (S) and one or more other elements, such as lead (Pb) in the mineral galena, or antimony (Sb) in the mineral stibnite.

NATIVE ELEMENTS

Dendritic (branching) copper

Limonite groundmass (matrix)

COPPER
(Cu)

SULFIDES

Dendritic (branching) gold

White diamond

Kimberlite groundmass (matrix)

Quartz vein

Hexagonal graphite crystal

GOLD
(Au)

DIAMOND
(C)

GRAPHITE
(C)

Cubic galena crystal

OXIDES/HYDROXIDES

Rounded bauxite grains in groundmass (matrix)

Milky quartz groundmass (matrix)

Smoky quartz crystal

Mass of specular hematite crystals

GALENA
(PbS)

SMOKY QUARTZ
(SiO_2)

SPECULAR HEMATITE
(Fe_2O_3)

Prismatic stibnite crystal

BAUXITE
($FeO(OH)$ and $Al_2O_3 2H_2O$)

Quartz groundmass (matrix)

STIBNITE
(Sb_2S_3)

Perfect octahedral pyrites crystal

Quartz crystal

Specular crystals of hematite

Kidney ore hematite

Parallel bands of onyx

PYRITES
(FeS_2)

ONYX
(SiO_2)

KIDNEY ORE HEMATITE
(Fe_2O_3)

PHOSPHATES

Limonite groundmass (matrix)

Rock groundmass (matrix)

Radiating wavellite crystals

Prismatic pyromorphite crystals

PYROMORPHITE
$(Pb_5(PO_4)_3Cl)$

WAVELLITE
$(Al_3(PO_4)_2(OH,F)_3.5H_2O)$

CARBONATES

Striated cerussite crystal

Dog tooth calcite crystal

CERUSSITE
$(PbCO_3)$

CALCITE
$(CaCO_3)$

SULFATES

Rock groundmass (matrix)

Radiating crystal mass of daisy gypsum

Radiating cyanotrichite crystals

CYANOTRICHITE
$(Cu_4Al_2(SO_4)(OH)_{12}.2H_2O)$

DAISY GYPSUM
$(CaSO_4.2H_2O)$

MOLYBDATE

Tabular wulfenite crystal

Dark rock groundmass (matrix)

WULFENITE
$(PbMoO_4)$

SILICATES

Feldspar groundmass (matrix)

Transparent bicolored tourmaline crystal

Dodecahedral sodalite crystal

SODALITE
$(Na_8Al_6Si_6O_{24}Cl_2)$

Striated surface of olivine crystal

TOURMALINE
$(Na(Mg,Fe,Li,Mn,Al)_3Al_6(BO_3)_5Si_6.O_{18}(OH,F)_4)$

OLIVINE
$(Fe_2SiO_4 - Mg_2SiO_4)$

Striated prismatic epidote crystal

Tabular muscovite crystal

EPIDOTE
$(Ca_2(Al,Fe)_3(SiO_4)_3(OH))$

Orthoclase crystal

MUSCOVITE
$(KAl_2(Si_3Al)O_{10}(OH,F)_2)$

ORTHOCLASE
$(KAlSi_3O_8)$

HALIDES

Cubic rock salt crystal

Cubic fluorite crystal

GREEN FLUORITE
(CaF_2)

ORANGE HALITE (ROCK SALT)
$(NaCl)$

Mineral features

MINERALS CAN BE IDENTIFIED BY STUDYING features such as fracture, cleavage, crystal system, habit, hardness, color, and streak. Minerals can break in different ways. If a mineral breaks in an irregular way, leaving rough surfaces, it possesses fracture. If a mineral breaks along well-defined planes of weakness, it possesses cleavage. Specific minerals have distinctive patterns of cleavage. For example, mica cleaves along one plane. Most minerals form crystals that can be categorized into crystal systems according to their symmetry and number of faces. Within each system, several different but related forms of crystal are possible; for example, a cubic crystal can have six, eight, or twelve sides. A mineral's habit is the typical form taken by an aggregate of its crystals. Examples of habit include botryoidal (like a bunch of grapes) and massive (no definite form). The relative hardness of a mineral may be assessed by testing its resistance to scratching. This property is usually measured using Mohs' scale, which increases in hardness from 1 (talc) to 10 (diamond). The color of a mineral is not a dependable guide to its identity as some minerals have a range of colors. Streak (the color the powdered mineral makes when rubbed across an unglazed tile) is a more reliable indicator.

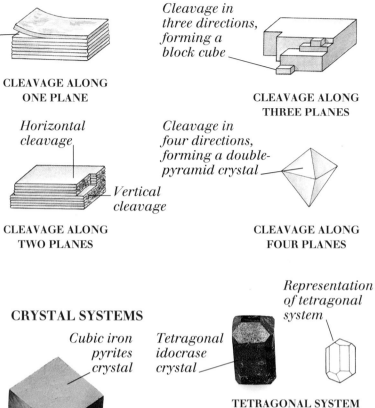

CLEAVAGE

Cleavage in one direction

CLEAVAGE ALONG ONE PLANE

Cleavage in three directions, forming a block cube

CLEAVAGE ALONG THREE PLANES

Horizontal cleavage

Vertical cleavage

CLEAVAGE ALONG TWO PLANES

Cleavage in four directions, forming a double-pyramid crystal

CLEAVAGE ALONG FOUR PLANES

CRYSTAL SYSTEMS

Cubic iron pyrites crystal

Tetragonal idocrase crystal

Representation of tetragonal system

TETRAGONAL SYSTEM

CUBIC SYSTEM

Representation of cubic system

Hexagonal beryl crystal

Representation of hexagonal/trigonal system

HEXAGONAL/TRIGONAL SYSTEM

Orthorhombic barite crystal

Representation of orthorhombic system

ORTHORHOMBIC SYSTEM

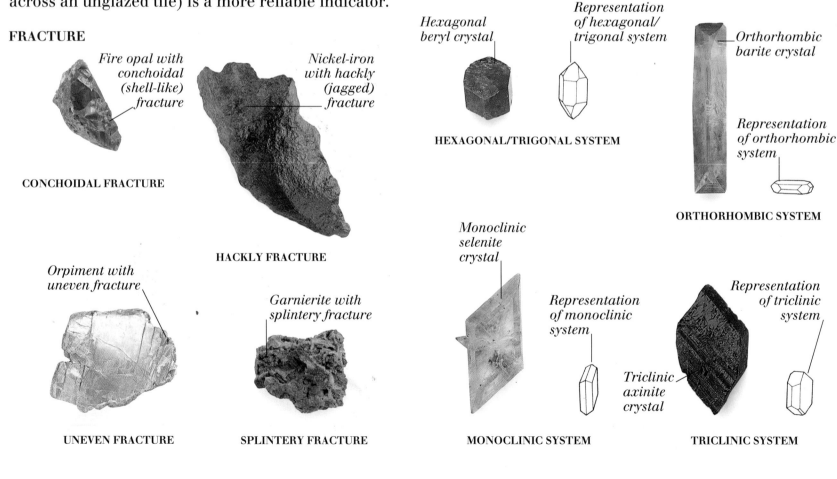

FRACTURE

Fire opal with conchoidal (shell-like) fracture

Nickel-iron with hackly (jagged) fracture

CONCHOIDAL FRACTURE

HACKLY FRACTURE

Orpiment with uneven fracture

Garnierite with splintery fracture

Monoclinic selenite crystal

Representation of monoclinic system

Representation of triclinic system

Triclinic axinite crystal

UNEVEN FRACTURE

SPLINTERY FRACTURE

MONOCLINIC SYSTEM

TRICLINIC SYSTEM

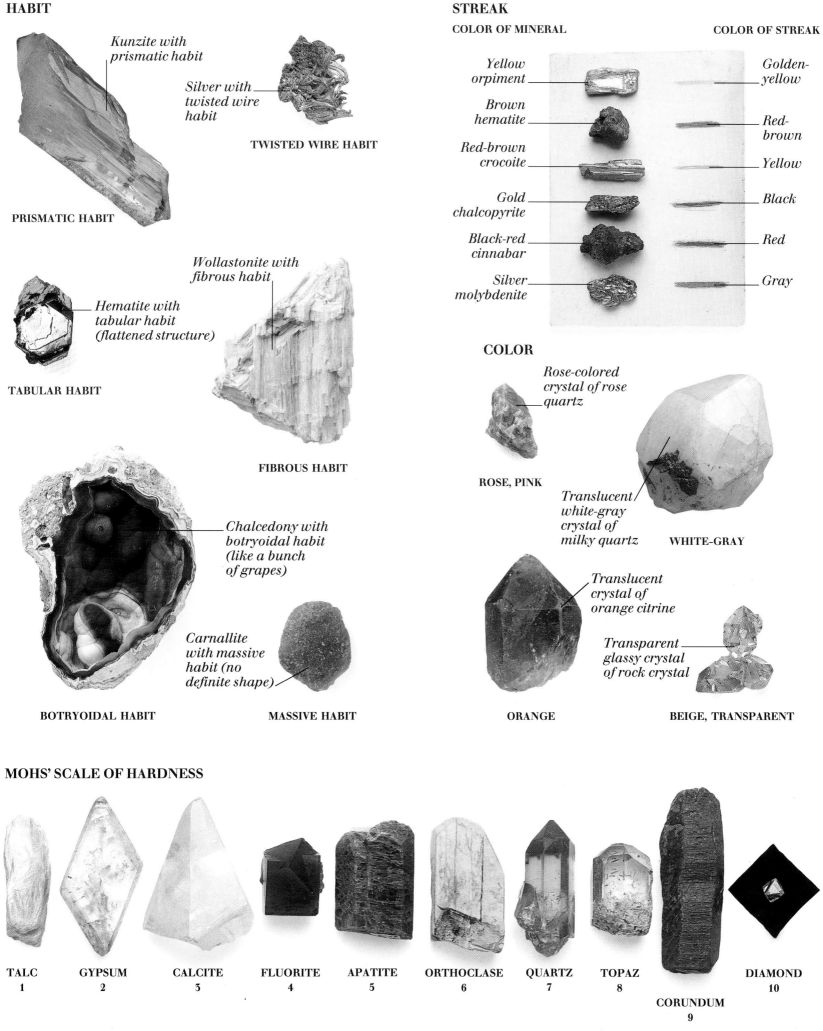

HABIT

Kunzite with prismatic habit

Silver with twisted wire habit

TWISTED WIRE HABIT

PRISMATIC HABIT

Wollastonite with fibrous habit

Hematite with tabular habit (flattened structure)

TABULAR HABIT

FIBROUS HABIT

Chalcedony with botryoidal habit (like a bunch of grapes)

Carnallite with massive habit (no definite shape)

BOTRYOIDAL HABIT

MASSIVE HABIT

STREAK

COLOR OF MINERAL

COLOR OF STREAK

Yellow orpiment

Golden-yellow

Brown hematite

Red-brown

Red-brown crocoite

Yellow

Gold chalcopyrite

Black

Black-red cinnabar

Red

Silver molybdenite

Gray

COLOR

Rose-colored crystal of rose quartz

Translucent white-gray crystal of milky quartz

ROSE, PINK

WHITE-GRAY

Translucent crystal of orange citrine

Transparent glassy crystal of rock crystal

ORANGE

BEIGE, TRANSPARENT

MOHS' SCALE OF HARDNESS

| TALC | GYPSUM | CALCITE | FLUORITE | APATITE | ORTHOCLASE | QUARTZ | TOPAZ | | DIAMOND |
| 1 | 2 | 3 | 4 | 5 | 6 | 7 | 8 | | 10 |

CORUNDUM
9

Igneous and metamorphic rocks

IGNEOUS ROCKS ARE FORMED WHEN MAGMA (molten rock that originates from deep beneath the Earth's crust) cools and solidifies. There are two main types of igneous rock: intrusive and extrusive. Intrusive rocks are formed deep underground, where magma is forced into cracks or between rock layers to form structures including sills, dikes, and batholiths. The magma cools slowly to form coarse-grained rocks such as gabbro and pegmatite. Extrusive rocks are formed above the Earth's surface from lava (magma that has been ejected in a volcanic eruption). The molten lava cools quickly, producing fine-grained rocks such as rhyolite and basalt. Metamorphic rocks are those that have been altered by intense heat (contact metamorphism) or extreme pressure (regional metamorphism). Contact metamorphism occurs when rocks are changed by heat from, for example, an igneous intrusion or lava flow. Regional metamorphism occurs when rock is crushed in the middle of a folding mountain range. Metamorphic rocks can be formed from igneous rocks, sedimentary rocks, or even other metamorphic rocks.

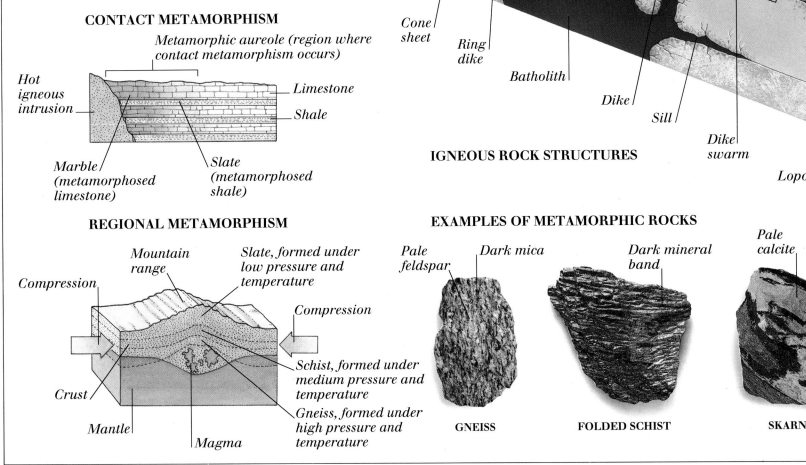

CONTACT METAMORPHISM

Metamorphic aureole (region where contact metamorphism occurs)

Hot igneous intrusion

Limestone

Shale

Marble (metamorphosed limestone)

Slate (metamorphosed shale)

IGNEOUS ROCK STRUCTURES

Butte

Plug

Cedar tree laccolith

Cinder cone

Large eroded lava flow

Cone sheet

Ring dike

Batholith

Dike

Sill

Dike swarm

Lopolith

REGIONAL METAMORPHISM

Mountain range

Slate, formed under low pressure and temperature

Compression

Compression

Crust

Mantle

Magma

Schist, formed under medium pressure and temperature

Gneiss, formed under high pressure and temperature

EXAMPLES OF METAMORPHIC ROCKS

Pale feldspar

Dark mica

Dark mineral band

Pale calcite

GNEISS

FOLDED SCHIST

SKARN

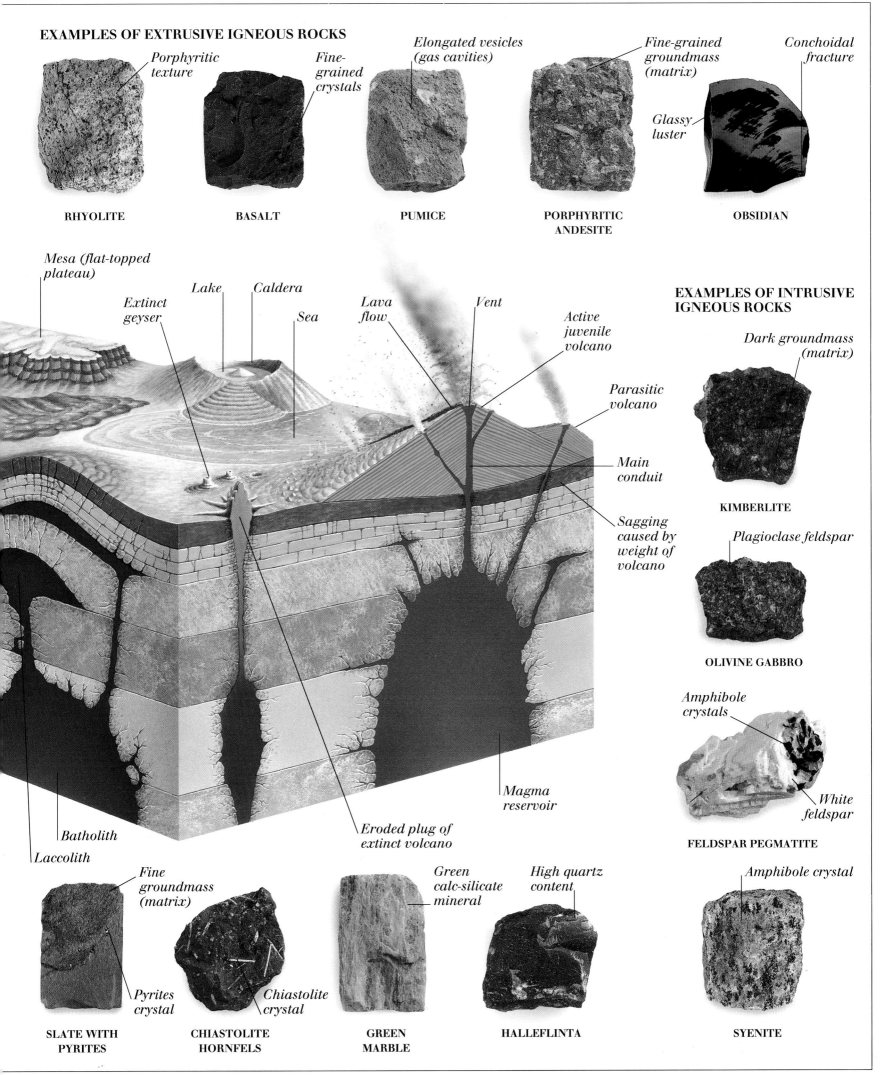

EXAMPLES OF EXTRUSIVE IGNEOUS ROCKS

Porphyritic texture

Fine-grained crystals

Elongated vesicles (gas cavities)

Fine-grained groundmass (matrix)

Conchoidal fracture

Glassy luster

RHYOLITE

BASALT

PUMICE

PORPHYRITIC ANDESITE

OBSIDIAN

Mesa (flat-topped plateau)

Extinct geyser

Lake

Caldera

Sea

Lava flow

Vent

Active juvenile volcano

Parasitic volcano

Main conduit

Sagging caused by weight of volcano

Magma reservoir

Eroded plug of extinct volcano

Batholith

Laccolith

EXAMPLES OF INTRUSIVE IGNEOUS ROCKS

Dark groundmass (matrix)

KIMBERLITE

Plagioclase feldspar

OLIVINE GABBRO

Amphibole crystals

White feldspar

FELDSPAR PEGMATITE

Fine groundmass (matrix)

Pyrites crystal

Chiastolite crystal

Green calc-silicate mineral

High quartz content

Amphibole crystal

SLATE WITH PYRITES

CHIASTOLITE HORNFELS

GREEN MARBLE

HALLEFLINTA

SYENITE

Sedimentary rocks

SEDIMENTARY ROCKS ARE FORMED BY THE ACCUMULATION and consolidation of sediments (see pp. 20-21). There are three main types of sedimentary rock: clastic sedimentary rocks, such as breccia or sandstone, are formed from other rocks that have been broken down into fragments by weathering (see pp. 34-35), which have then been transported and deposited elsewhere; organic sedimentary rocks, such as coal (see pp. 32-33), are derived from plant and animal remains; and chemical sedimentary rocks are formed by chemical processes. For example, rock salt is formed when salt dissolved in water is deposited as the water evaporates. Sedimentary rocks are laid down in layers called beds, or strata. Each new layer is laid down horizontally over older ones. There are usually some gaps in the sequence, called unconformities. These represent periods in which no new sediments were being laid down, or when earlier sedimentary layers were raised above sea level and eroded away.

THE GRAND CANYON, U.S.A.

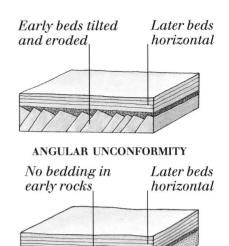

EXAMPLES OF UNCONFORMITIES

Early beds tilted and eroded   Later beds horizontal

ANGULAR UNCONFORMITY

No bedding in early rocks   Later beds horizontal

NONCONFORMITY

Early beds folded and eroded   Later beds horizontal

DISCONFORMITY

SEDIMENTARY LAYERS OF THE GRAND CANYON REGION

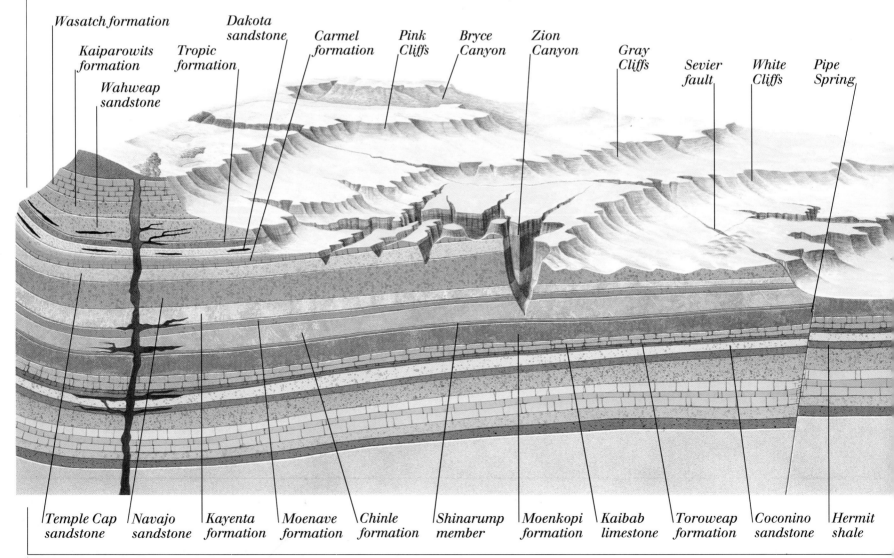

Wasatch formation
Kaiparowits formation
Wahweap sandstone
Tropic formation
Dakota sandstone
Carmel formation
Pink Cliffs
Bryce Canyon
Zion Canyon
Gray Cliffs
Sevier fault
White Cliffs
Pipe Spring

Temple Cap sandstone | Navajo sandstone | Kayenta formation | Moenave formation | Chinle formation | Shinarump member | Moenkopi formation | Kaibab limestone | Toroweap formation | Coconino sandstone | Hermit shale

EXAMPLES OF SEDIMENTARY ROCKS

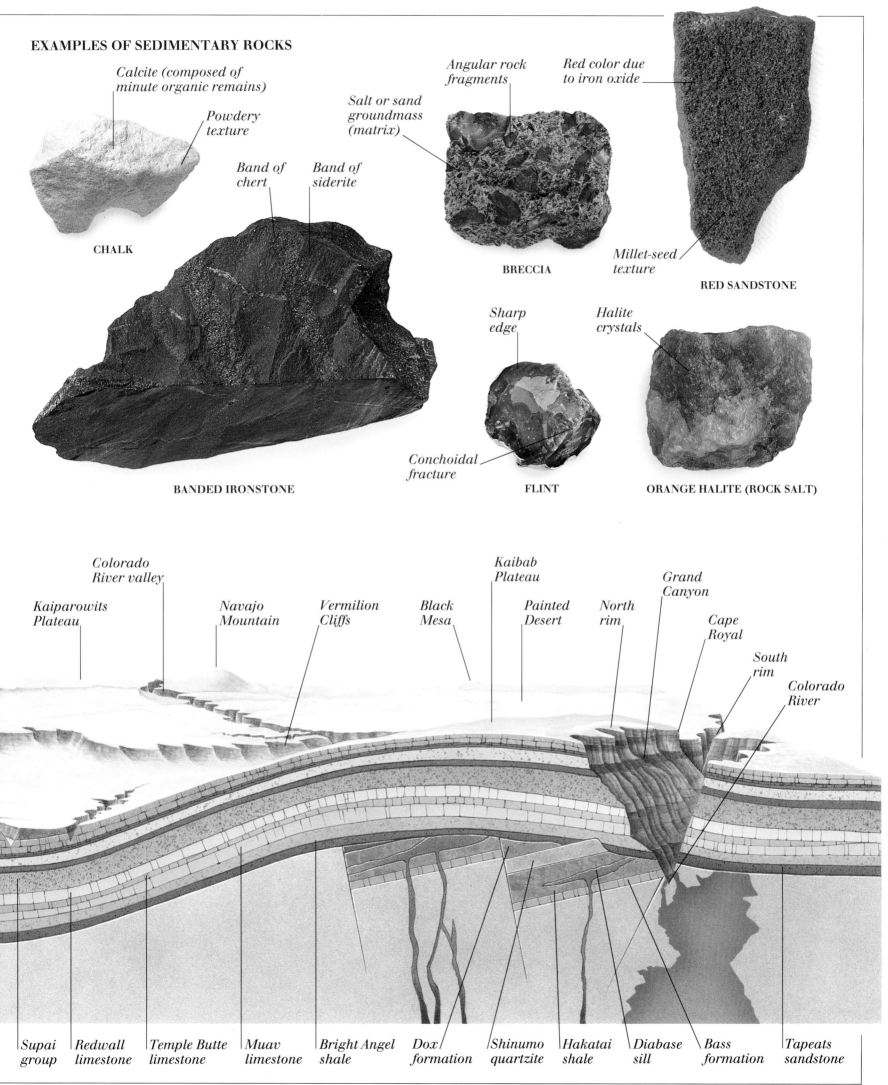

Calcite (composed of minute organic remains)

Powdery texture

CHALK

Band of chert

Band of siderite

BANDED IRONSTONE

Angular rock fragments

Salt or sand groundmass (matrix)

BRECCIA

Red color due to iron oxide

Millet-seed texture

RED SANDSTONE

Sharp edge

Conchoidal fracture

FLINT

Halite crystals

ORANGE HALITE (ROCK SALT)

Kaiparowits Plateau

Colorado River valley

Navajo Mountain

Vermilion Cliffs

Black Mesa

Kaibab Plateau

Painted Desert

North rim

Grand Canyon

Cape Royal

South rim

Colorado River

Supai group

Redwall limestone

Temple Butte limestone

Muav limestone

Bright Angel shale

Dox formation

Shinumo quartzite

Hakatai shale

Diabase sill

Bass formation

Tapeats sandstone

Fossils

FOSSILS ARE THE REMAINS of plants and animals that have been preserved in rock. A fossil may be the preserved remains of an organism itself, an impression of it in rock, or preserved traces (known as trace fossils) left by an organism while it was alive, such as organic carbon outlines, fossilized footprints, or droppings. Most dead organisms soon rot away or are eaten by scavengers. For fossilization to occur, rapid burial by sediment is necessary. The organism decays, but the harder parts—bones, teeth, and shells, for example—may be preserved and hardened by minerals from the surrounding sediment. Fossilization may also occur even when the hard parts of an organism are dissolved away to leave an impression called a mold. The mold is filled by minerals, thereby creating a cast of the organism. The study of fossils (paleontology) not only can show how living things have evolved, but can also help reveal the Earth's geological history—for example, by aiding in the dating of rock strata.

PROCESS OF FOSSILIZATION

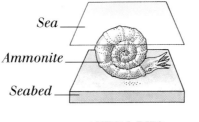

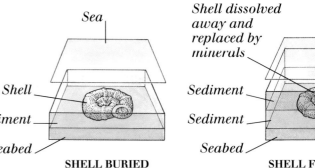

ANIMAL DIES

SOFT PARTS ROT

SHELL BURIED

SHELL FOSSILIZED

EXAMPLES OF FOSSILS

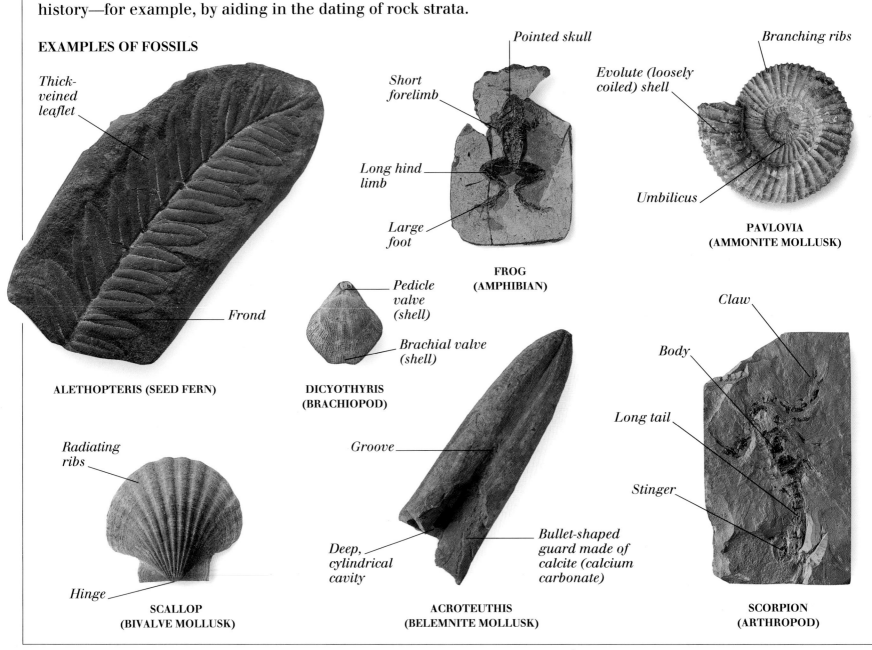

ALETHOPTERIS (SEED FERN)

Thick-veined leaflet

Frond

Radiating ribs

Hinge

SCALLOP
(BIVALVE MOLLUSK)

Pedicle valve (shell)

Brachial valve (shell)

DICYOTHYRIS
(BRACHIOPOD)

Pointed skull

Short forelimb

Long hind limb

Large foot

FROG
(AMPHIBIAN)

Groove

Deep, cylindrical cavity

Bullet-shaped guard made of calcite (calcium carbonate)

ACROTEUTHIS
(BELEMNITE MOLLUSK)

Branching ribs

Evolute (loosely coiled) shell

Umbilicus

PAVLOVIA
(AMMONITE MOLLUSK)

Claw

Body

Long tail

Stinger

SCORPION
(ARTHROPOD)

30

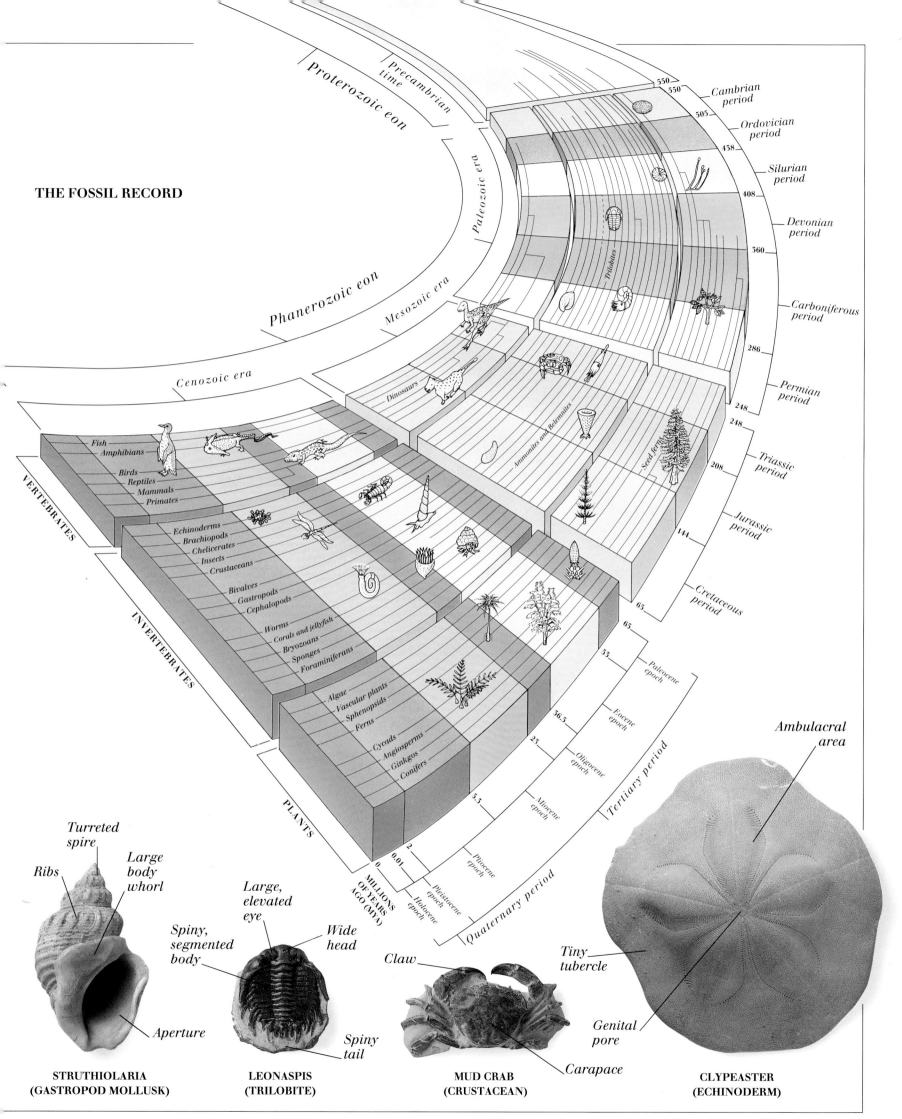

THE FOSSIL RECORD

Precambrian time

Proterozoic eon

Paleozoic era

Phanerozoic eon

Mesozoic era

Cenozoic era

550

550 — Cambrian period

505 — Ordovician period

438 — Silurian period

408 — Devonian period

360 — Carboniferous period

Trilobites

286 — Permian period

248 — Triassic period

Ammonites and Belemnites

Seed fern

208 — Jurassic period

144 — Cretaceous period

Dinosaurs

65

65 — Paleocene epoch

53 — Eocene epoch

36.5 — Oligocene epoch

25 — Miocene epoch

Tertiary period

5.3 — Pliocene epoch

2 — Pleistocene epoch

0.01 — Holocene epoch

Quaternary period

MILLIONS OF YEARS AGO (MYA)

0

VERTEBRATES

Fish
Amphibians
Birds
Reptiles
Mammals
Primates

INVERTEBRATES

Echinoderms
Brachiopods
Chelicerates
Insects
Crustaceans
Bivalves
Gastropods
Cephalopods
Worms
Corals and jellyfish
Bryozoans
Sponges
Foraminiferans

PLANTS

Algae
Vascular plants
Sphenopsids
Ferns
Cycads
Angiosperms
Ginkgos
Conifers

Turreted spire

Ribs

Large body whorl

Aperture

**STRUTHIOLARIA
(GASTROPOD MOLLUSK)**

Large, elevated eye

Spiny, segmented body

Wide head

Spiny tail

**LEONASPIS
(TRILOBITE)**

Claw

Carapace

**MUD CRAB
(CRUSTACEAN)**

Ambulacral area

Tiny tubercle

Genital pore

**CLYPEASTER
(ECHINODERM)**

Mineral resources

MINERAL RESOURCES CAN BE DEFINED AS naturally occurring substances that can be extracted from the Earth and are useful as fuels and raw materials. Coal, oil, and gas—collectively called fossil fuels—are commonly included in this group, but are not strictly minerals, because they are of organic origin. Coal formation begins when vegetation is buried and partly decomposed to form peat. Overlying sediments compress the peat and transform it into lignite (soft brown coal). As the overlying sediments accumulate, increasing pressure and temperature eventually transform the lignite into bituminous and hard anthracite coals. Oil and gas are usually formed from organic molecules that were deposited in marine sediments. Under the effects of heat and pressure, the compressed organic molecules undergo complex chemical changes to form oil and gas. The oil and gas percolate upward through water-saturated permeable rocks. They may rise to the Earth's surface, or accumulate below an impermeable layer of rock that has been folded or faulted to form a trap—an anticline (upfold) trap, for example. Minerals are inorganic substances that may consist of a single chemical element, such as gold, silver, or copper, or combinations of elements (see pp. 22-23). Some minerals are concentrated in mineralization zones in rock associated with crustal movements or volcanic activity. Others may be found in sediments as placer deposits—accumulations of high-density minerals that have been weathered out of rocks, transported, and deposited (on riverbeds, for example).

OIL RIG, NORTH SEA

Stalk

Leaf

PLANT MATTER

Decayed plant matter

About 60% carbon

PEAT

About 70% carbon

Crumbly texture

LIGNITE (BROWN COAL)

Powdery texture

About 80% carbon

Shiny surface

BITUMINOUS COAL

About 95% carbon

HOW COAL IS FORMED

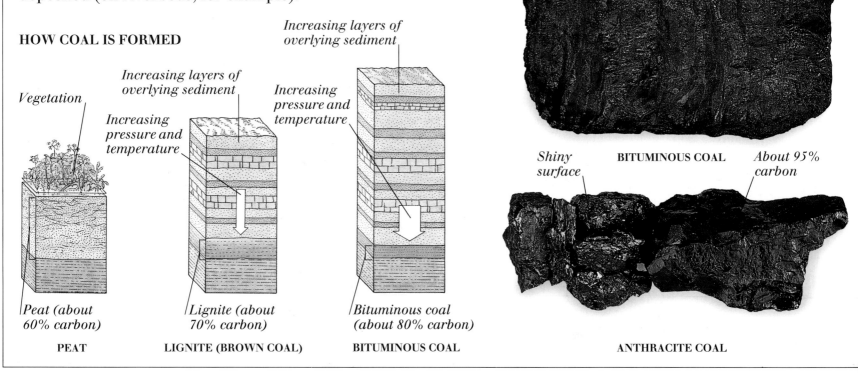

Vegetation

Increasing layers of overlying sediment

Increasing pressure and temperature

Increasing layers of overlying sediment

Increasing pressure and temperature

Peat (about 60% carbon)

Lignite (about 70% carbon)

Bituminous coal (about 80% carbon)

PEAT

LIGNITE (BROWN COAL)

BITUMINOUS COAL

ANTHRACITE COAL

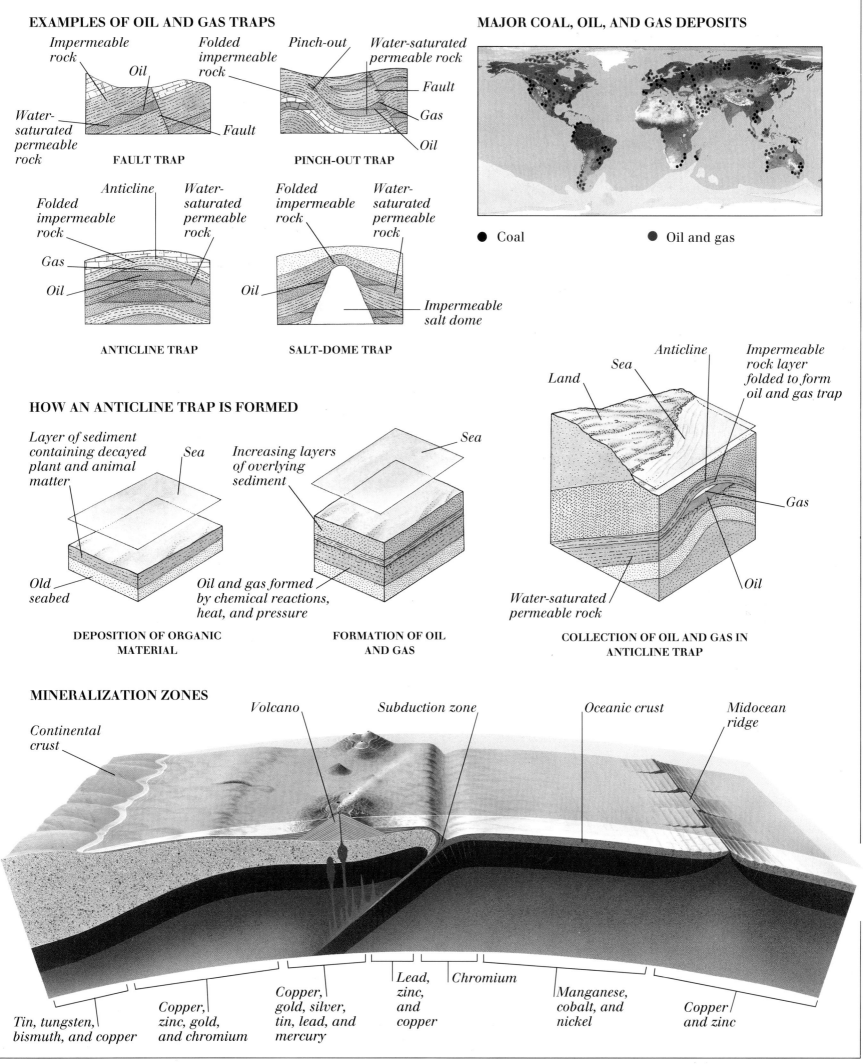

EXAMPLES OF OIL AND GAS TRAPS

FAULT TRAP

Impermeable rock
Oil
Folded impermeable rock
Water-saturated permeable rock
Fault

PINCH-OUT TRAP

Pinch-out
Water-saturated permeable rock
Fault
Gas
Oil

ANTICLINE TRAP

Folded impermeable rock
Anticline
Water-saturated permeable rock
Gas
Oil

SALT-DOME TRAP

Folded impermeable rock
Water-saturated permeable rock
Oil
Impermeable salt dome

MAJOR COAL, OIL, AND GAS DEPOSITS

● Coal
● Oil and gas

HOW AN ANTICLINE TRAP IS FORMED

DEPOSITION OF ORGANIC MATERIAL

Layer of sediment containing decayed plant and animal matter
Sea
Old seabed

FORMATION OF OIL AND GAS

Increasing layers of overlying sediment
Sea
Oil and gas formed by chemical reactions, heat, and pressure

COLLECTION OF OIL AND GAS IN ANTICLINE TRAP

Land
Sea
Anticline
Impermeable rock layer folded to form oil and gas trap
Gas
Oil
Water-saturated permeable rock

MINERALIZATION ZONES

Continental crust
Volcano
Subduction zone
Oceanic crust
Midocean ridge

Tin, tungsten, bismuth, and copper
Copper, zinc, gold, and chromium
Copper, gold, silver, tin, lead, and mercury
Lead, zinc, and copper
Chromium
Manganese, cobalt, and nickel
Copper and zinc

Weathering and erosion

WEATHERING IS THE BREAKING DOWN of rocks on the Earth's surface. There are two main types: physical (or mechanical), and chemical. Physical weathering may be caused by temperature changes, such as freezing and thawing, or by abrasion from material carried by winds, rivers, or glaciers. Rocks may also be broken down by the actions of animals and plants, such as the burrowing of animals and the growth of roots. Chemical weathering causes rocks to decompose by changing their chemical composition. For example, rainwater may dissolve certain minerals in a rock. Erosion is the wearing away and removal of land surfaces by water, wind, or ice. It is greatest in areas of little or no surface vegetation, such as deserts, where sand dunes may form.

FORMATION OF A ROCK PAVEMENT (HAMADA)

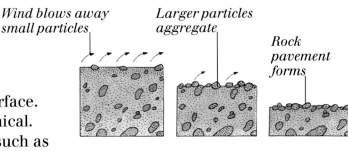

Wind blows away small particles

Larger particles aggregate

Rock pavement forms

FIRST STAGE

SECOND STAGE

FINAL STAGE

FEATURES OF WEATHERING AND EROSION

FEATURES PRODUCED BY WIND ACTION

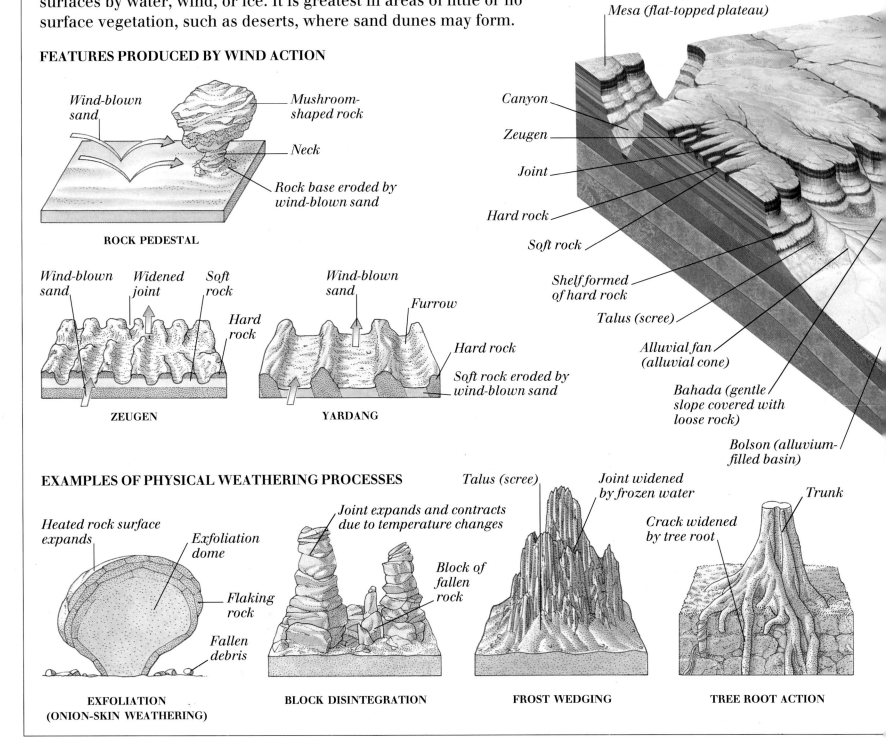

Wind-blown sand

Mushroom-shaped rock

Neck

Rock base eroded by wind-blown sand

ROCK PEDESTAL

Wind-blown sand *Widened joint* *Soft rock* *Hard rock*

ZEUGEN

Wind-blown sand *Furrow* *Hard rock* *Soft rock eroded by wind-blown sand*

YARDANG

Mesa (flat-topped plateau)

Canyon

Zeugen

Joint

Hard rock

Soft rock

Shelf formed of hard rock

Talus (scree)

Alluvial fan (alluvial cone)

Bahada (gentle slope covered with loose rock)

Bolson (alluvium-filled basin)

EXAMPLES OF PHYSICAL WEATHERING PROCESSES

Heated rock surface expands

Exfoliation dome

Flaking rock

Fallen debris

EXFOLIATION (ONION-SKIN WEATHERING)

Joint expands and contracts due to temperature changes

Block of fallen rock

BLOCK DISINTEGRATION

Talus (scree)

Joint widened by frozen water

FROST WEDGING

Crack widened by tree root

Trunk

TREE ROOT ACTION

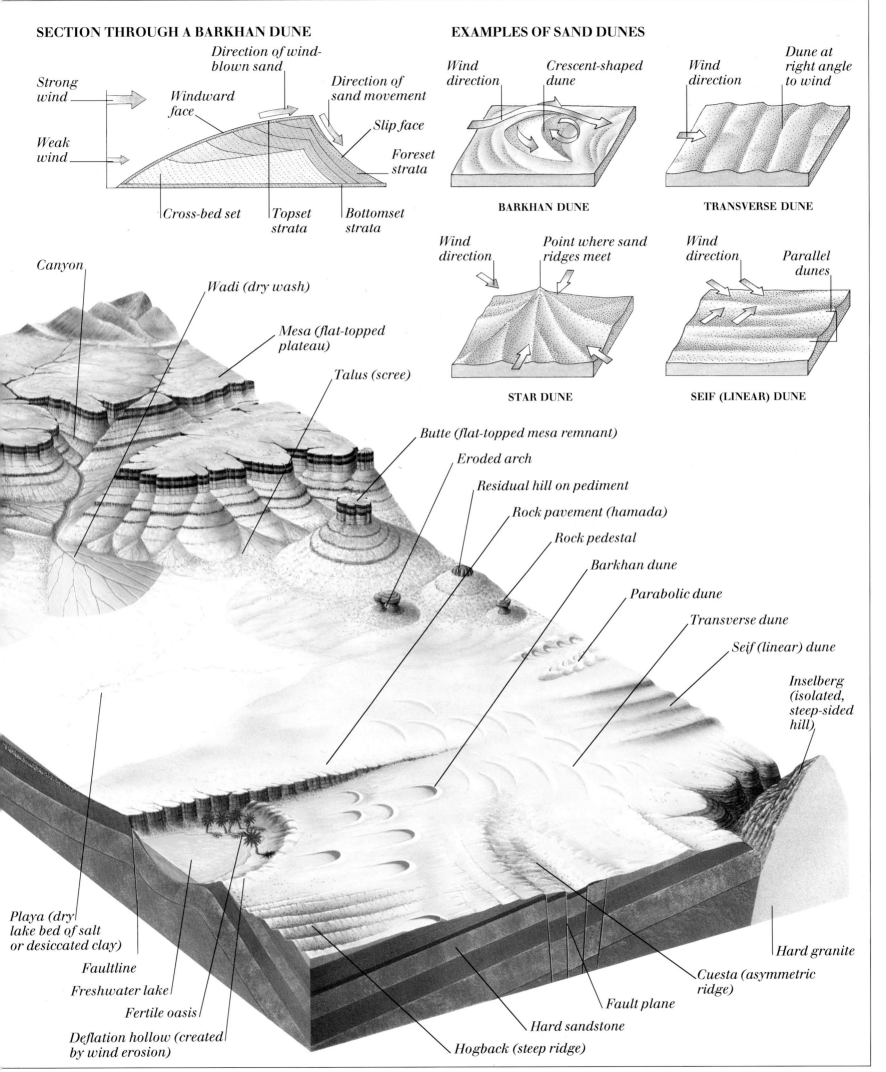

SECTION THROUGH A BARKHAN DUNE

Strong wind

Weak wind

Windward face

Direction of wind-blown sand

Direction of sand movement

Slip face

Foreset strata

Cross-bed set

Topset strata

Bottomset strata

EXAMPLES OF SAND DUNES

Wind direction

Crescent-shaped dune

BARKHAN DUNE

Wind direction

Dune at right angle to wind

TRANSVERSE DUNE

Wind direction

Point where sand ridges meet

STAR DUNE

Wind direction

Parallel dunes

SEIF (LINEAR) DUNE

Canyon

Wadi (dry wash)

Mesa (flat-topped plateau)

Talus (scree)

Butte (flat-topped mesa remnant)

Eroded arch

Residual hill on pediment

Rock pavement (hamada)

Rock pedestal

Barkhan dune

Parabolic dune

Transverse dune

Seif (linear) dune

Inselberg (isolated, steep-sided hill)

Playa (dry lake bed of salt or desiccated clay)

Faultline

Freshwater lake

Fertile oasis

Deflation hollow (created by wind erosion)

Hogback (steep ridge)

Hard sandstone

Fault plane

Cuesta (asymmetric ridge)

Hard granite

Caves

CAVES COMMONLY FORM in areas of limestone, although on coastlines they also occur in other rocks. Limestone is made of calcite (calcium carbonate), which dissolves in the carbonic acid naturally present in rainwater, and in humic acids from the decay of vegetation. The acidic water trickles down through cracks and joints in the limestone and between rock layers, breaking up the surface terrain into clints (blocks of rock), separated by grikes (deep cracks), and punctuated by sinkholes (also called swallow holes or potholes) into which surface streams may disappear. Underground, the acidic water dissolves the rock around crevices, opening up a network of passages and caves, which can become large caverns if the roofs collapse. Various features are formed when the dissolved calcite is redeposited. For example, it may be redeposited along an underground stream to form a gour (series of calcite ridges), or in caves and passages to form stalactites and stalagmites. Stalactites develop where calcite is left behind as water drips from the roof; where the drops land, stalagmites build up.

MERGED STALACTITE

STALACTITE WITH RING MARKS

Ring mark

SURFACE TOPOGRAPHY OF A CAVE SYSTEM

Doline (depression caused by collapse of cave roof)

Sinkhole

Porous limestone

Gorge where cave roof has fallen in

Resurgence

Limestone terrain with clints and grikes

Impermeable rock

STALAGMITE FORMATIONS

Calcite (calcium carbonate) crystalized under water

Thin encrustations of calcite (calcium carbonate)

CRYSTALLINE STALAGMITIC FLOOR

CALCAREOUS TUFA

Encrustations on dead stems of small plants

Calcite (calcium carbonate)

Calcite (calcium carbonate)

STALAGMITIC FLOOR

Calcite (calcium carbonate)

Encrustations with fungoid structure

STALAGMITIC BOSS

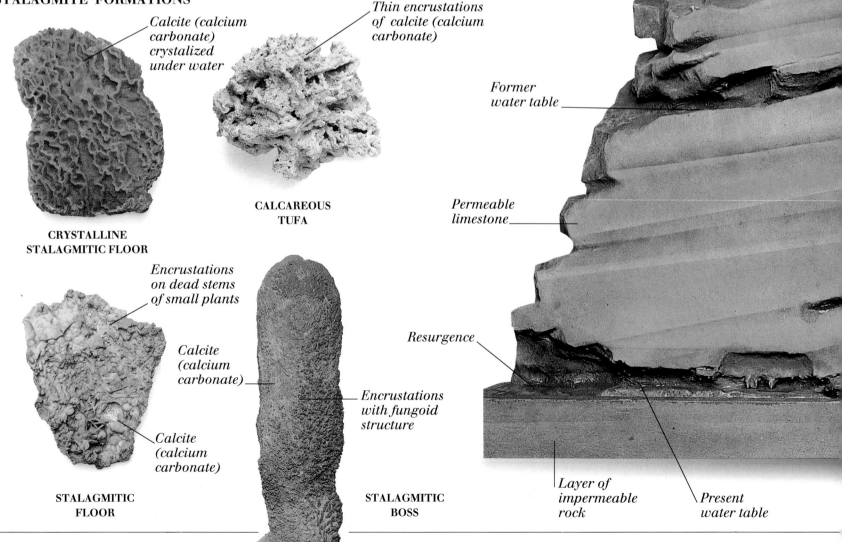

Scar of bare rock

Former water table

Permeable limestone

Resurgence

Layer of impermeable rock

Present water table

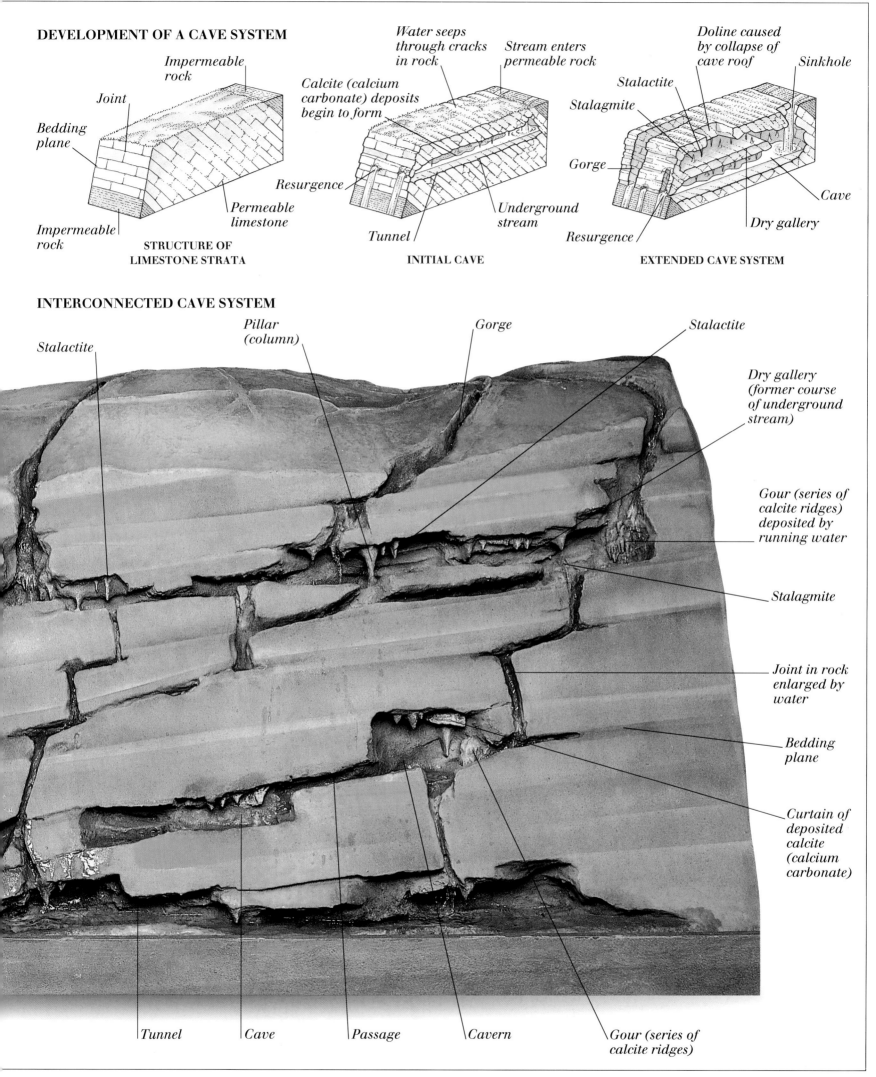

DEVELOPMENT OF A CAVE SYSTEM

STRUCTURE OF LIMESTONE STRATA

Impermeable rock

Joint

Bedding plane

Impermeable rock

Permeable limestone

INITIAL CAVE

Water seeps through cracks in rock

Stream enters permeable rock

Calcite (calcium carbonate) deposits begin to form

Resurgence

Tunnel

Underground stream

EXTENDED CAVE SYSTEM

Doline caused by collapse of cave roof

Sinkhole

Stalactite

Stalagmite

Gorge

Resurgence

Cave

Dry gallery

INTERCONNECTED CAVE SYSTEM

Stalactite

Pillar (column)

Gorge

Stalactite

Dry gallery (former course of underground stream)

Gour (series of calcite ridges) deposited by running water

Stalagmite

Joint in rock enlarged by water

Bedding plane

Curtain of deposited calcite (calcium carbonate)

Tunnel

Cave

Passage

Cavern

Gour (series of calcite ridges)

Glaciers

GLACIER BAY, ALASKA

A VALLEY GLACIER IS A LARGE MASS OF ICE that forms on land and moves slowly downhill under its own weight. It is formed from snow that collects in cirques (mountain hollows also known as corries), compressing into ice as more and more snow accumulates. The cirque is deepened by frost wedging and abrasion (see pp. 34-35), and arêtes (sharp ridges) develop between adjacent cirques. Eventually, so much ice builds up that the glacier begins to flow. As the glacier moves it collects moraine (debris), which may range in size from particles of dust to large boulders. The rocks at the base of the glacier erode the glacial valley, giving it a U-shaped cross section. Under the glacier, *roches moutonnées* (eroded outcrops of hard rock) and drumlins (rounded mounds of rock and clay) are left behind on the valley floor. The glacier ends at a terminus (the snout), where the ice melts as fast as it arrives. If the temperature increases, the ice melts faster than it arrives, and the glacier retreats. The retreating glacier leaves behind its moraine and also erratics (isolated single boulders). Glacial streams from the melting glacier deposit eskers and kames (ridges and mounds of sand and gravel) but carry away the finer sediment to form a stratified outwash plain. Lumps of ice carried on to this plain melt, creating holes called kettles.

VALLEY GLACIER

POST-GLACIAL VALLEY

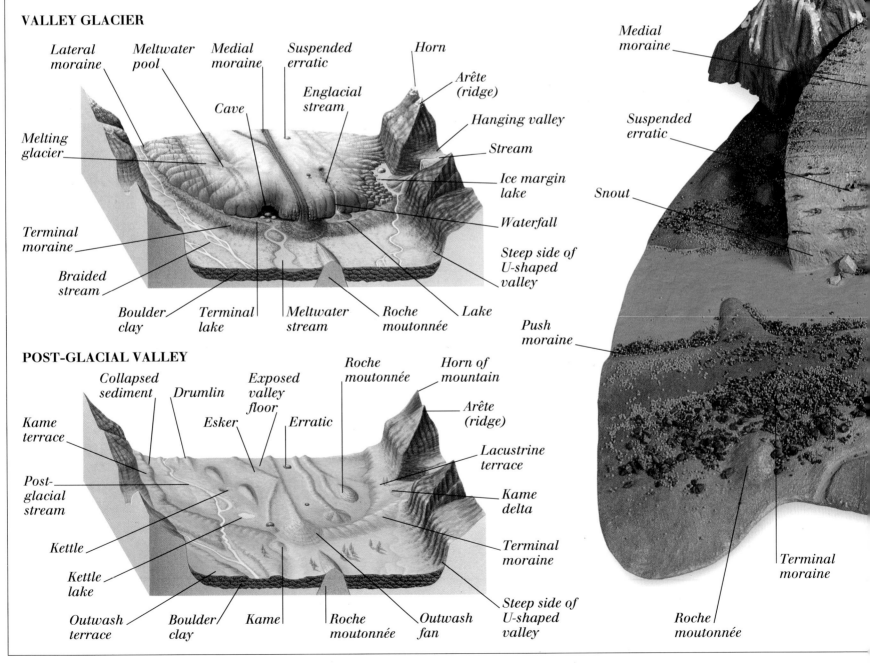

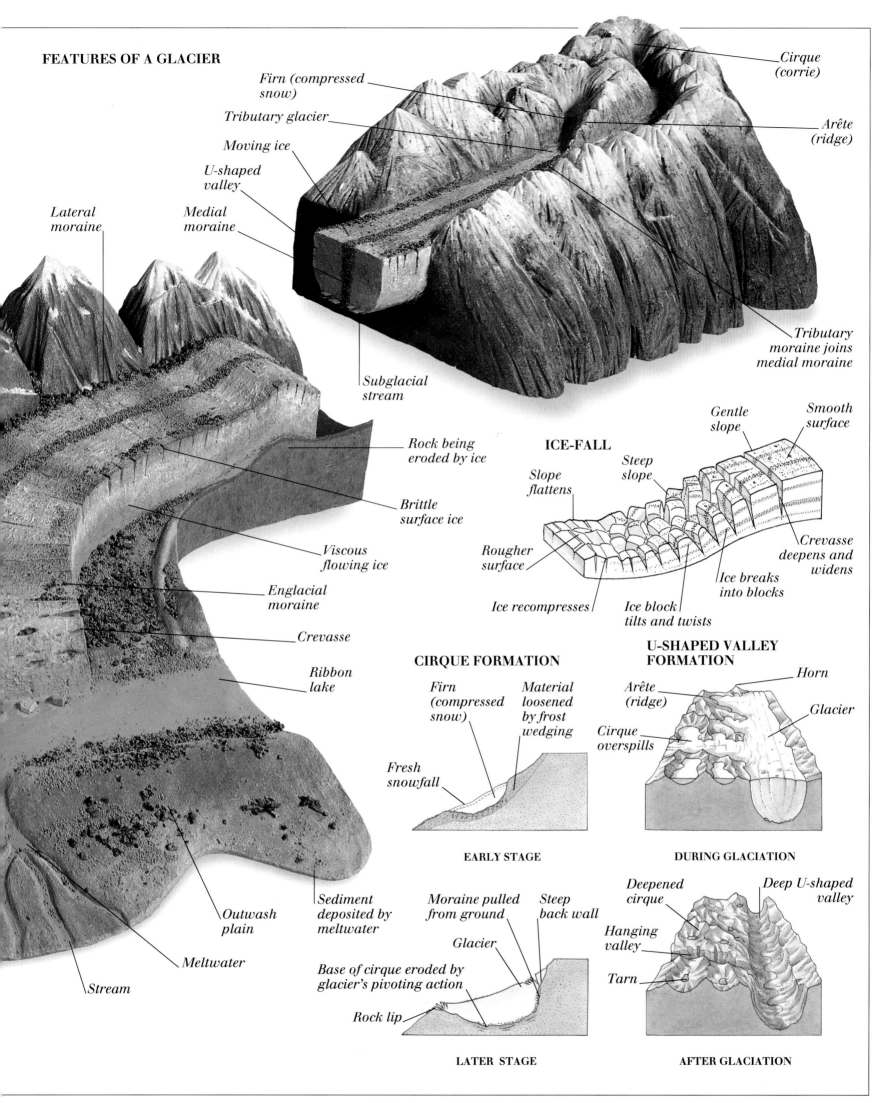

FEATURES OF A GLACIER

Firn (compressed snow)

Tributary glacier

Moving ice

U-shaped valley

Medial moraine

Lateral moraine

Subglacial stream

Cirque (corrie)

Arête (ridge)

Tributary moraine joins medial moraine

Rock being eroded by ice

Brittle surface ice

Viscous flowing ice

Englacial moraine

Crevasse

Ribbon lake

Sediment deposited by meltwater

Outwash plain

Meltwater

Stream

ICE-FALL

Gentle slope

Smooth surface

Steep slope

Slope flattens

Rougher surface

Ice recompresses

Ice block tilts and twists

Ice breaks into blocks

Crevasse deepens and widens

CIRQUE FORMATION

Firn (compressed snow)

Material loosened by frost wedging

Fresh snowfall

EARLY STAGE

Moraine pulled from ground

Steep back wall

Glacier

Base of cirque eroded by glacier's pivoting action

Rock lip

LATER STAGE

U-SHAPED VALLEY FORMATION

Horn

Arête (ridge)

Glacier

Cirque overspills

DURING GLACIATION

Deepened cirque

Deep U-shaped valley

Hanging valley

Tarn

AFTER GLACIATION

Rivers

RIVERS FORM PART of the water cycle—the continuous circulation of water between the land, sea, and atmosphere. The source of a river may be a mountain spring, or lake, or a melting glacier. The course that the river subsequently takes depends on the slope of the terrain and on the rock types and formations over which it flows. In its early, upland stages, a river tumbles steeply over rocks and boulders, and cuts a steep-sided V-shaped valley. Farther downstream, it flows smoothly over sediments and forms winding meanders, eroding sideways to create broad valleys and plains. On reaching the coast, the river may deposit sediment, forming an estuary or delta (see pp. 42-43).

RIVER CAPTURE

Tributary erodes headward

River

River

EARLY STAGE

Dry valley

River captured by tributary

River flow decreases

River flow increases

LATER STAGE

THE WATER CYCLE

Precipitation falls on high ground

Wind

Water carried downstream by river

Water vapor released into atmosphere by trees and other plants

Wind

Water vapor forms clouds

Water evaporates from sea

Water stored in sea

River flows into sea

Water seeps underground and flows to sea

Water evaporates from lake

Water seeps underground and flows to sea

SATELLITE IMAGE OF GANGES RIVER DELTA, BANGLADESH

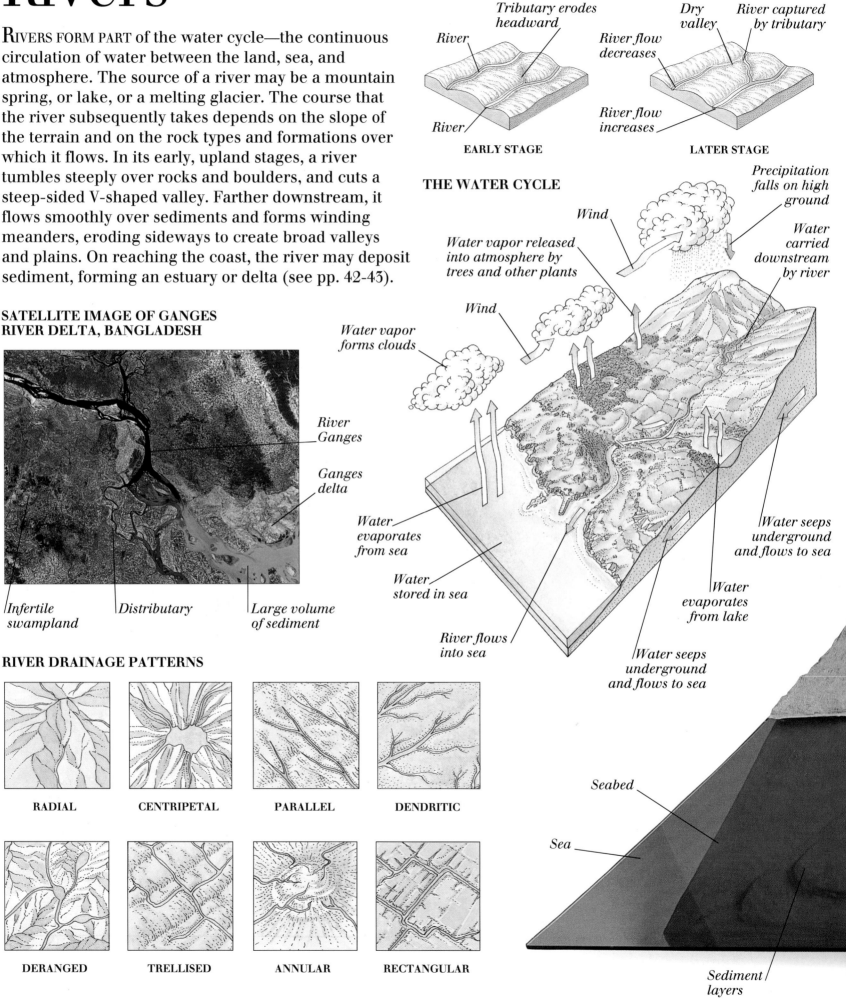

River Ganges

Ganges delta

Infertile swampland

Distributary

Large volume of sediment

Seabed

Sea

Sediment layers

RIVER DRAINAGE PATTERNS

RADIAL

CENTRIPETAL

PARALLEL

DENDRITIC

DERANGED

TRELLISED

ANNULAR

RECTANGULAR

STAGES IN A RIVER'S DEVELOPMENT

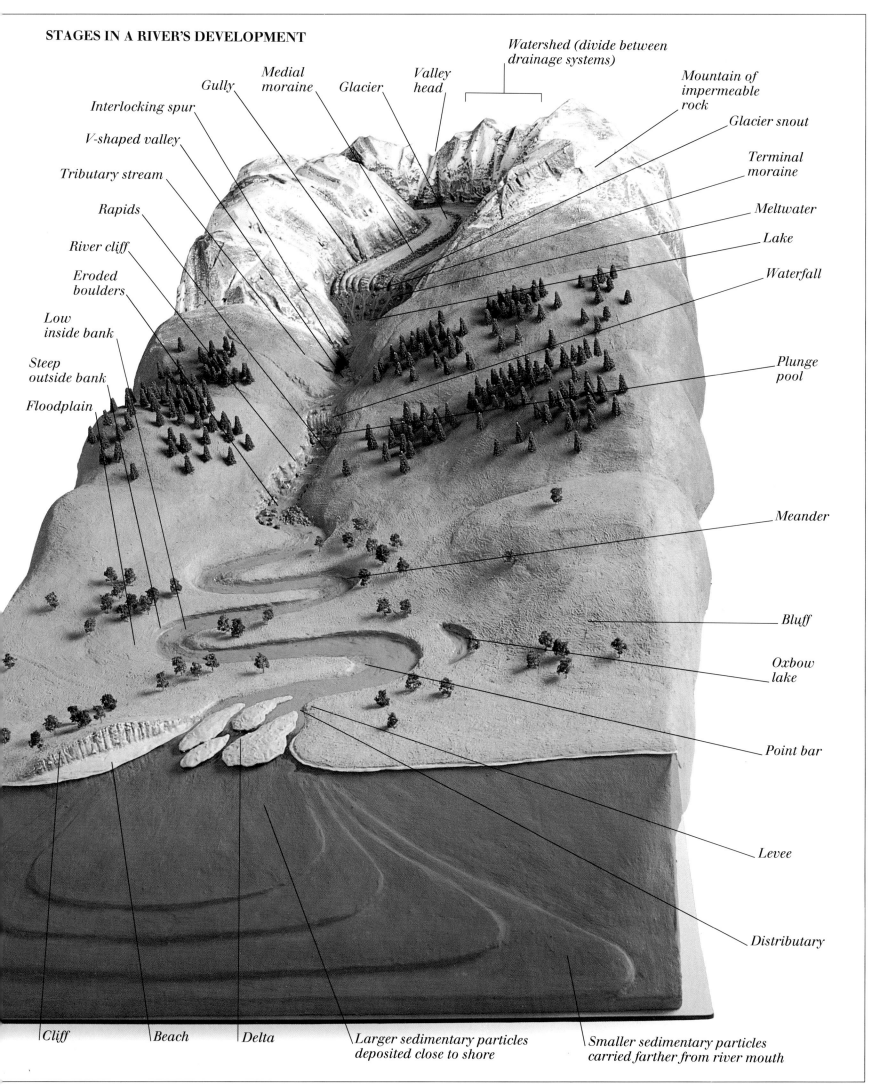

Gully

Medial moraine

Glacier

Valley head

Watershed (divide between drainage systems)

Mountain of impermeable rock

Glacier snout

Terminal moraine

Meltwater

Lake

Waterfall

Plunge pool

Meander

Bluff

Oxbow lake

Point bar

Levee

Distributary

Interlocking spur

V-shaped valley

Tributary stream

Rapids

River cliff

Eroded boulders

Low inside bank

Steep outside bank

Floodplain

Cliff

Beach

Delta

Larger sedimentary particles deposited close to shore

Smaller sedimentary particles carried farther from river mouth

River features

RIVERS ARE ONE OF THE MAJOR FORCES that shape the landscape. Near its source, a river is steep (see pp. 40-41). It erodes downward, carving out V-shaped valleys and deep gorges. Waterfalls and rapids are formed where the river flows from hard rock to softer, more easily eroded rock. Farther downstream, meanders may form and there is greater sideways erosion, resulting in a broad river valley. The river sometimes erodes through the neck of a meander to form an oxbow lake. Sediment deposited on the valley floor by meandering rivers and during floods helps to create a floodplain. Floods may also deposit sediment on the banks of the river to form levees. As a river spills into the sea or a lake, it deposits large amounts of sediment, and may form a delta. A delta is an area of sand bars, swamps and lagoons through which the river flows in several channels called distributaries—the Mississippi delta, for example. Often, a rise in sea level may have flooded the river mouth to form a broad estuary, a tidal section where seawater mixes with fresh water.

HOW WATERFALLS AND RAPIDS ARE FORMED

Plunge pool

Hard rock

Softer rock

WATERFALL

Hard rock

River erodes softer rocks to form rapids

Softer rock

Gently sloping rock strata

RAPIDS

A RIVER VALLEY DRAINAGE SYSTEM

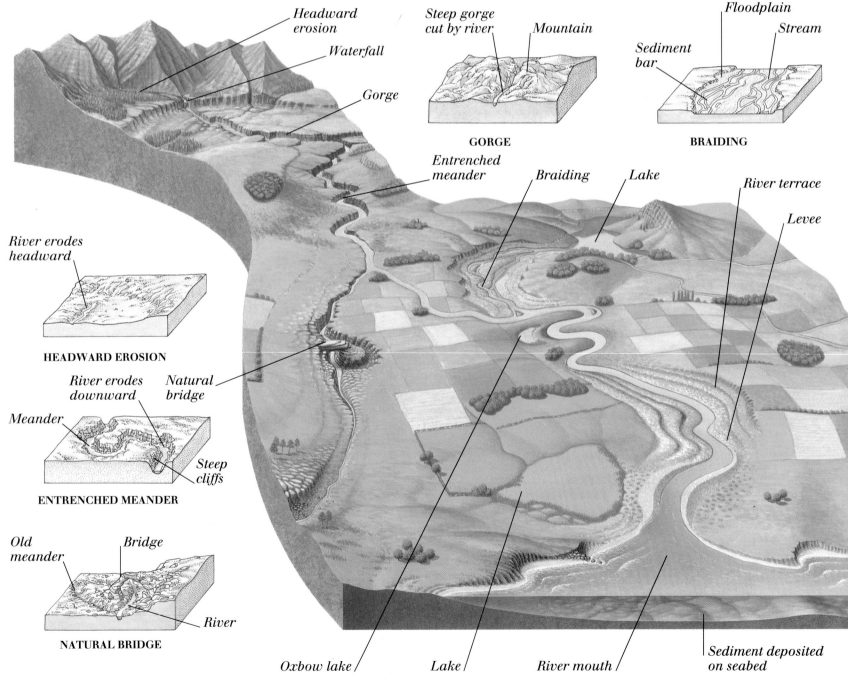

Headward erosion

Waterfall

Gorge

Steep gorge cut by river

Mountain

GORGE

Floodplain

Stream

Sediment bar

BRAIDING

Entrenched meander

Braiding

Lake

River terrace

Levee

River erodes headward

HEADWARD EROSION

River erodes downward

Natural bridge

Meander

Steep cliffs

ENTRENCHED MEANDER

Old meander

Bridge

River

NATURAL BRIDGE

Oxbow lake

Lake

River mouth

Sediment deposited on seabed

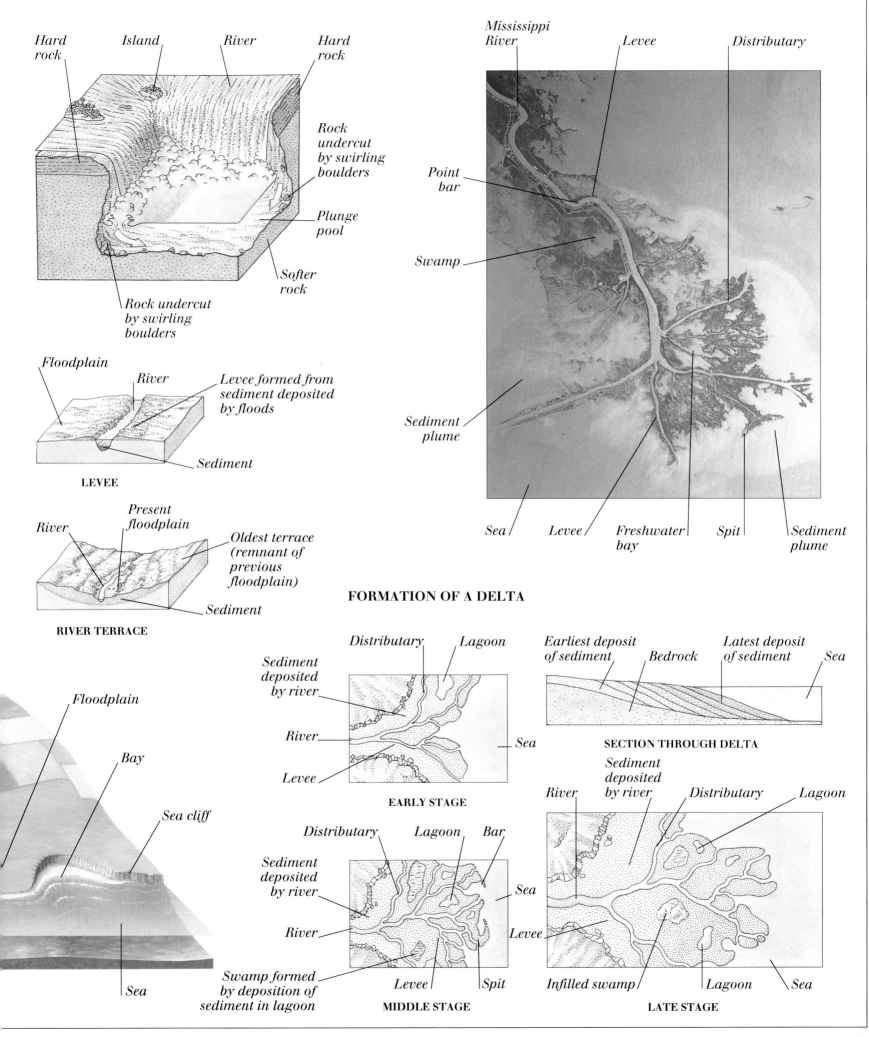

WATERFALL FEATURES

Hard rock

Island

River

Hard rock

Rock undercut by swirling boulders

Plunge pool

Softer rock

Rock undercut by swirling boulders

Floodplain

River

Levee formed from sediment deposited by floods

Sediment

LEVEE

River

Present floodplain

Oldest terrace (remnant of previous floodplain)

Sediment

RIVER TERRACE

Floodplain

Bay

Sea cliff

Sea

THE MISSISSIPPI DELTA

Mississippi River

Levee

Distributary

Point bar

Swamp

Sediment plume

Sea

Levee

Freshwater bay

Spit

Sediment plume

FORMATION OF A DELTA

Distributary

Lagoon

Sediment deposited by river

River

Sea

Levee

EARLY STAGE

Earliest deposit of sediment

Bedrock

Latest deposit of sediment

Sea

SECTION THROUGH DELTA

Distributary

Lagoon

Bar

Sediment deposited by river

River

Sea

Levee

Spit

Swamp formed by deposition of sediment in lagoon

MIDDLE STAGE

Sediment deposited by river

River

Distributary

Lagoon

Levee

Infilled swamp

Lagoon

Sea

LATE STAGE

43

Lakes and groundwater

NATURAL LAKES OCCUR WHERE a large quantity of water collects in a hollow in impermeable rock or is prevented from draining away by a barrier, such as moraine (glacial deposits) or solidified lava. Lakes are often relatively short-lived landscape features, because they tend to become silted up by sediment from the streams and rivers that feed them. Some of the more

LAKE BAIKAL, RUSSIA

long-lasting lakes are found in deep rift valleys formed by vertical movements of the Earth's crust (see pp. 12-13)— for example, Lake Baikal in Russia, the world's largest freshwater lake, and the Dead Sea in the Middle East, one of the world's saltiest lakes. Where water is able to drain away, it sinks into the ground until it reaches a layer of impermeable rock, then accumulates in the permeable rock above it. This water-saturated permeable rock is called an aquifer. The saturated zone varies in depth according to seasonal and climatic changes. In wet conditions, the water stored underground builds up, while in dry periods it becomes depleted. Where the upper edge of the saturated zone—the water table—meets the ground surface, water emerges as springs. In an artesian basin, where the aquifer is below an aquiclude (layer of impermeable rock), the water table throughout the basin is determined by its height at the rim. At the center of such a basin, the water table is above ground level. The water in the basin is thus trapped below the water table and can rise under its own pressure along faultlines or well shafts.

STRUCTURE OF AN ARTESIAN BASIN

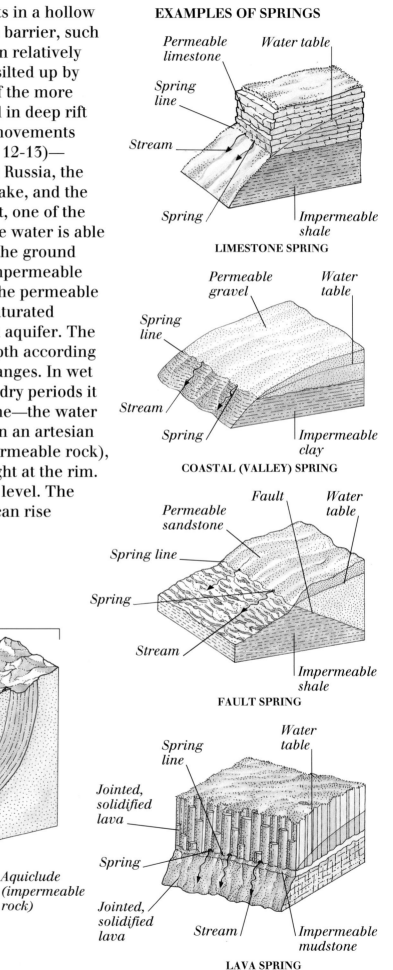

EXAMPLES OF SPRINGS

FEATURES OF A GROUNDWATER SYSTEM

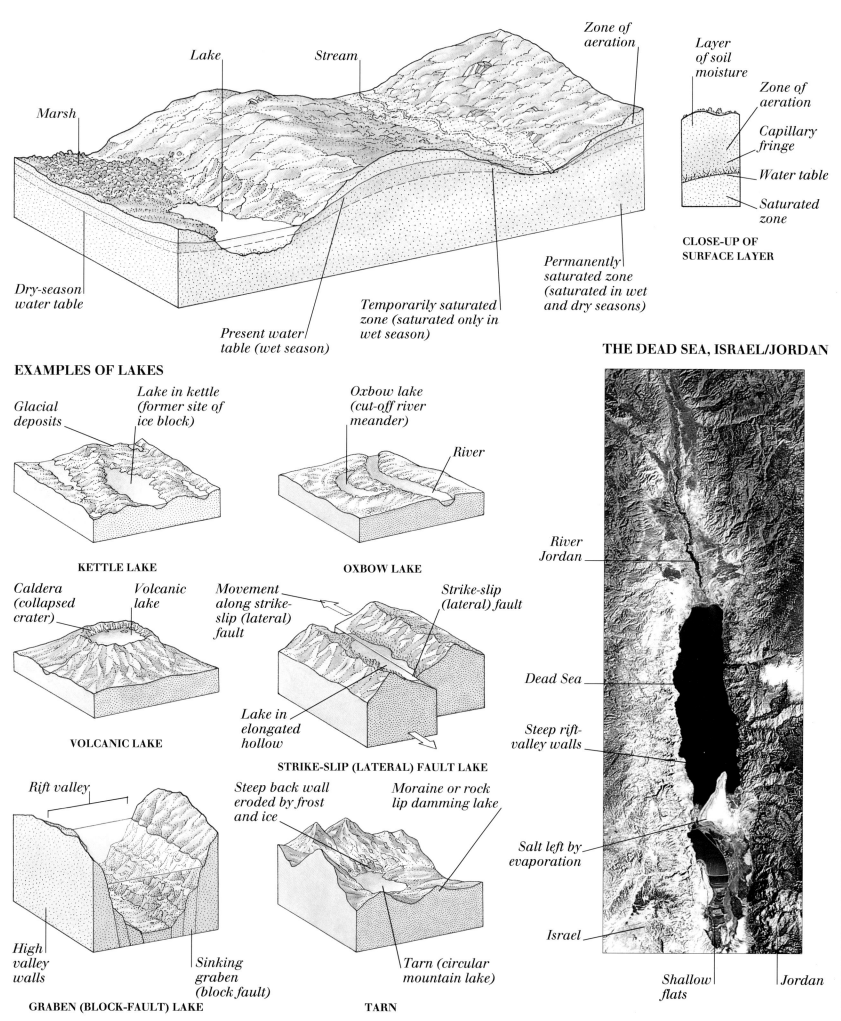

Marsh

Lake

Stream

Zone of aeration

Layer of soil moisture

Zone of aeration

Capillary fringe

Water table

Saturated zone

Dry-season water table

Present water table (wet season)

Temporarily saturated zone (saturated only in wet season)

Permanently saturated zone (saturated in wet and dry seasons)

CLOSE-UP OF SURFACE LAYER

EXAMPLES OF LAKES

Glacial deposits

Lake in kettle (former site of ice block)

Oxbow lake (cut-off river meander)

River

KETTLE LAKE

OXBOW LAKE

Caldera (collapsed crater)

Volcanic lake

Movement along strike-slip (lateral) fault

Strike-slip (lateral) fault

Lake in elongated hollow

VOLCANIC LAKE

STRIKE-SLIP (LATERAL) FAULT LAKE

Rift valley

Steep back wall eroded by frost and ice

Moraine or rock lip damming lake

High valley walls

Sinking graben (block fault)

Tarn (circular mountain lake)

GRABEN (BLOCK-FAULT) LAKE

TARN

THE DEAD SEA, ISRAEL/JORDAN

River Jordan

Dead Sea

Steep rift-valley walls

Salt left by evaporation

Israel

Shallow flats

Jordan

Coastlines

COASTLINES ARE AMONG THE MOST RAPIDLY changing landscape features. Some are eroded by waves, wind, and rain, causing cliffs to be undercut and caves to be hollowed out of solid rock. Others are built up by waves transporting sand and small rocks in a process known as longshore drift and by rivers depositing sediment in deltas. Additional influences include the activities of living organisms such as coral, crustal movements, and sea-level variations due to climatic changes. Rising land or a drop in sea level creates an emergent coastline, with cliffs and beaches standing above the new shoreline. Sinking land or a rise in sea level produces a drowned coastline, typified by fjords (submerged glacial valleys) or submerged river valleys.

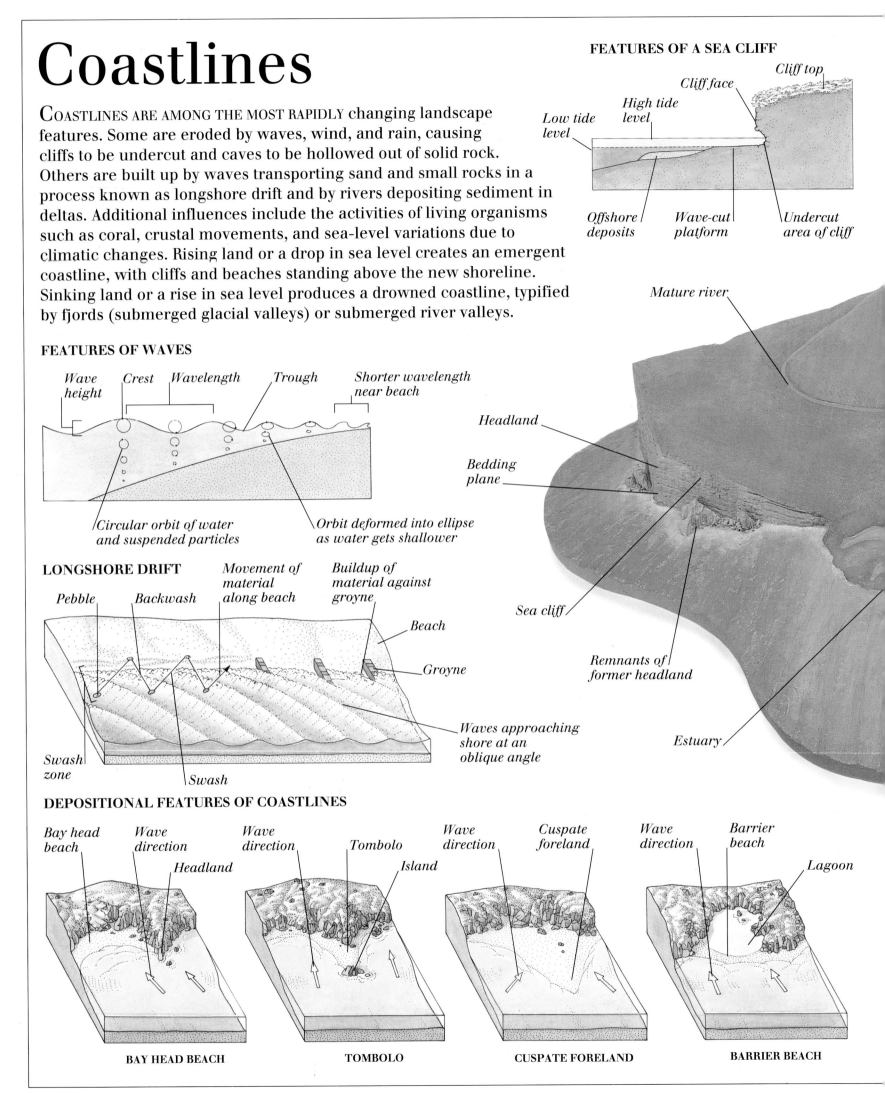

FEATURES OF A SEA CLIFF

Cliff top

Cliff face

High tide level

Low tide level

Offshore deposits

Wave-cut platform

Undercut area of cliff

Mature river

Headland

Bedding plane

Sea cliff

Remnants of former headland

Estuary

FEATURES OF WAVES

Wave height

Crest

Wavelength

Trough

Shorter wavelength near beach

Circular orbit of water and suspended particles

Orbit deformed into ellipse as water gets shallower

LONGSHORE DRIFT

Movement of material along beach

Buildup of material against groyne

Pebble

Backwash

Beach

Groyne

Swash zone

Swash

Waves approaching shore at an oblique angle

DEPOSITIONAL FEATURES OF COASTLINES

Bay head beach

Wave direction

Headland

Wave direction

Tombolo

Island

Wave direction

Cuspate foreland

Wave direction

Barrier beach

Lagoon

BAY HEAD BEACH

TOMBOLO

CUSPATE FORELAND

BARRIER BEACH

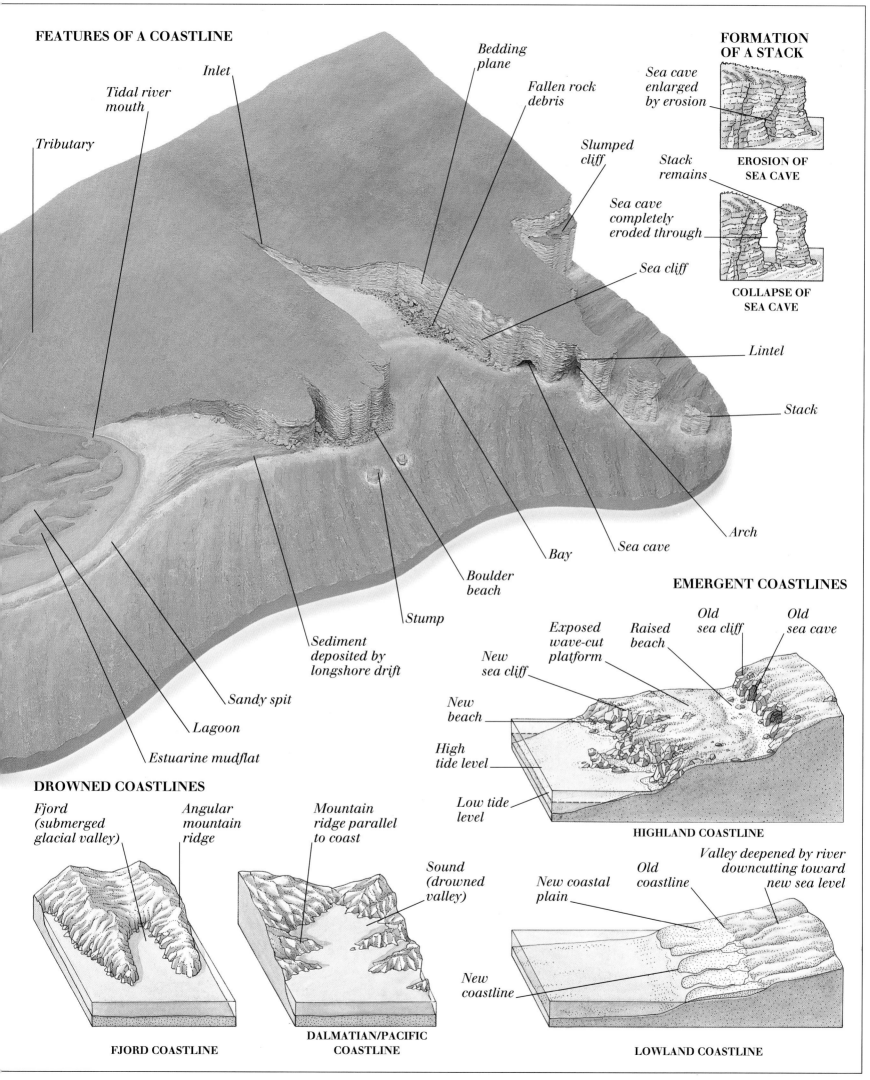

FEATURES OF A COASTLINE

Tidal river mouth

Inlet

Tributary

Bedding plane

Fallen rock debris

Slumped cliff

Sea cliff

Lintel

Stack

Arch

Sea cave

Bay

Boulder beach

Stump

Sediment deposited by longshore drift

Sandy spit

Lagoon

Estuarine mudflat

FORMATION OF A STACK

Sea cave enlarged by erosion

EROSION OF SEA CAVE

Stack remains

Sea cave completely eroded through

COLLAPSE OF SEA CAVE

EMERGENT COASTLINES

Old sea cliff

Old sea cave

Exposed wave-cut platform

Raised beach

New sea cliff

New beach

High tide level

Low tide level

HIGHLAND COASTLINE

DROWNED COASTLINES

Fjord (submerged glacial valley)

Angular mountain ridge

Mountain ridge parallel to coast

Sound (drowned valley)

Valley deepened by river downcutting toward new sea level

Old coastline

New coastal plain

New coastline

FJORD COASTLINE

DALMATIAN/PACIFIC COASTLINE

LOWLAND COASTLINE

Oceans and seas

OCEANS AND SEAS COVER ABOUT 70 PERCENT of the Earth's surface and account for about 97 percent of its total water. These oceans and seas play a crucial role in regulating temperature variations and determining climate. Their waters absorb heat from the Sun, especially in tropical regions, and the surface currents distribute it around the Earth, warming overlying air masses and neighboring land in winter and cooling them in summer. The oceans are never still. Differences in temperature and salinity drive deep current systems, while surface currents are generated by winds blowing over the oceans. All currents are deflected—to the right in the Northern Hemisphere, to the left in the Southern Hemisphere—as a result of the Earth's rotation. This deflective factor is known as the Coriolis force. A current that begins on the surface is immediately deflected. This current in turn generates a current in the layer of water beneath, which is also deflected. As the movement is transmitted downward, the deflections form an Ekman spiral. The waters of the oceans and seas are also moved by the constant ebb and flow of tides. These are caused by the gravitational pull of the Moon and Sun. The highest tides (Spring tides) occur at full and new Moon; the lowest tides (neap tides) occur at first and last quarter.

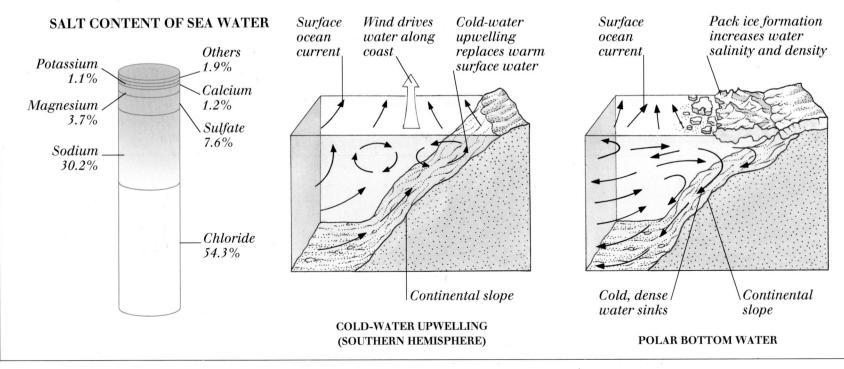

SALT CONTENT OF SEA WATER

Potassium 1.1%
Others 1.9%
Calcium 1.2%
Magnesium 3.7%
Sulfate 7.6%
Sodium 30.2%
Chloride 54.3%

Surface ocean current
Wind drives water along coast
Cold-water upwelling replaces warm surface water
Continental slope

COLD-WATER UPWELLING (SOUTHERN HEMISPHERE)

Surface ocean current
Pack ice formation increases water salinity and density
Cold, dense water sinks
Continental slope

POLAR BOTTOM WATER

OFFSHORE CURRENTS

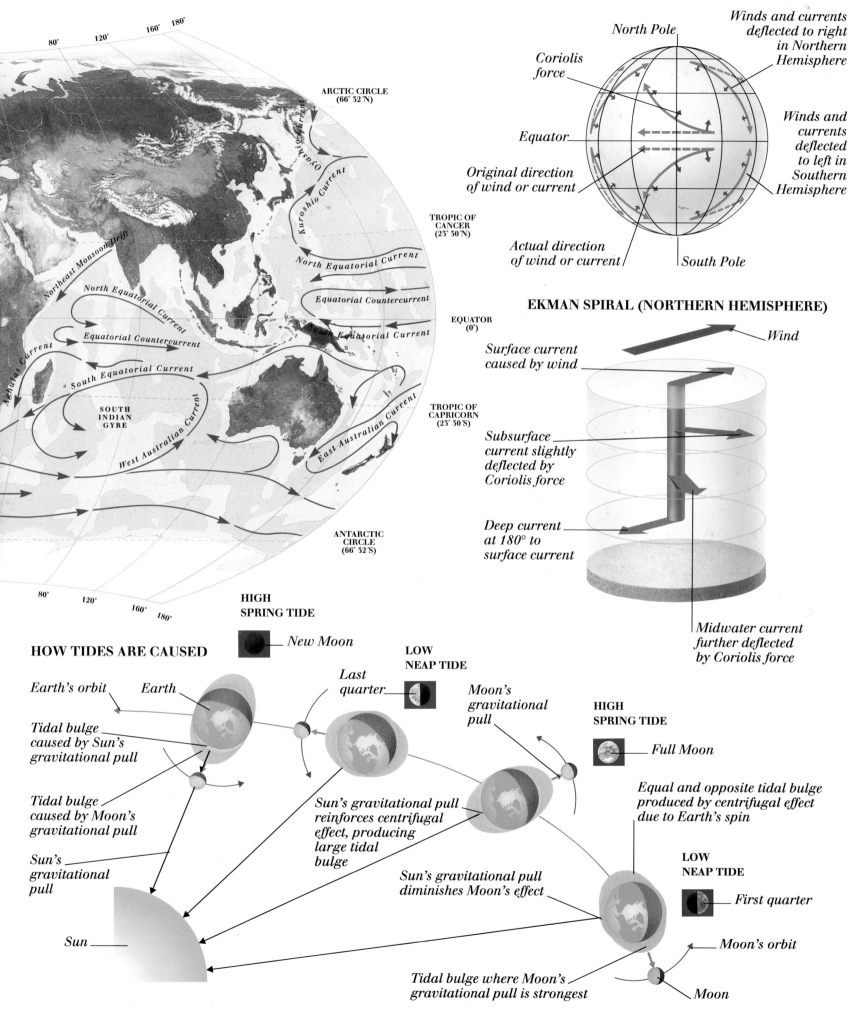

EFFECT OF CORIOLIS FORCE

Winds and currents deflected to right in Northern Hemisphere

North Pole

Coriolis force

Equator

Winds and currents deflected to left in Southern Hemisphere

Original direction of wind or current

Actual direction of wind or current

South Pole

ARCTIC CIRCLE (66° 32'N)

TROPIC OF CANCER (23° 30'N)

Oyashio Current

Kuroshio Current

Northeast Monsoon Drift

North Equatorial Current

North Equatorial Current

Equatorial Countercurrent

South Equatorial Current

Equatorial Countercurrent

South Equatorial Current

Agulhas Current

South Equatorial Current

SOUTH INDIAN GYRE

West Australian Current

East Australian Current

EQUATOR (0°)

TROPIC OF CAPRICORN (23° 30'S)

ANTARCTIC CIRCLE (66° 32'S)

80° 120° 160° 180°

80° 120° 160° 180°

EKMAN SPIRAL (NORTHERN HEMISPHERE)

Wind

Surface current caused by wind

Subsurface current slightly deflected by Coriolis force

Deep current at 180° to surface current

Midwater current further deflected by Coriolis force

HOW TIDES ARE CAUSED

HIGH SPRING TIDE

New Moon

LOW NEAP TIDE

Last quarter

Moon's gravitational pull

HIGH SPRING TIDE

Full Moon

Earth's orbit

Earth

Tidal bulge caused by Sun's gravitational pull

Tidal bulge caused by Moon's gravitational pull

Sun's gravitational pull

Sun's gravitational pull reinforces centrifugal effect, producing large tidal bulge

Equal and opposite tidal bulge produced by centrifugal effect due to Earth's spin

Sun's gravitational pull diminishes Moon's effect

LOW NEAP TIDE

First quarter

Sun

Moon's orbit

Tidal bulge where Moon's gravitational pull is strongest

Moon

49

The ocean floor

THE OCEAN FLOOR INCLUDES TWO SECTIONS: the continental shelf and slope, and the deep-ocean floor. The continental shelf and slope are part of the continental crust, but may extend far into the ocean. Sloping quite gently to a depth of about 460 feet, the continental shelf is covered in sandy deposits shaped by waves and tidal currents. At the edge of the continental shelf, the seabed slopes down to the abyssal plain, which lies at an average depth of about 12,500 feet. On this deep-ocean floor is a layer of sediment made up of clays, fine oozes formed from the remains of tiny sea creatures, and occasional mineral-rich deposits. Echo-sounding and remote sensing from satellites has revealed that the abyssal plain is divided by a world-circling system of mountain ranges, far bigger than any on land—the midocean ridge. Here, magma (molten rock) wells up from the Earth's interior and solidifies, widening the ocean floor (see pp. 12-13). As the ocean floor spreads, volcanoes that have formed over hot spots in the crust move away from their magma source; they become extinct and are increasingly submerged and eroded. Volcanoes eroded below sea level remain as seamounts (underwater mountains). In warm waters, a volcano that projects above the ocean surface often acquires a fringing coral reef, which may develop into an atoll as the volcano becomes submerged.

CONTINENTAL-SHELF FLOOR

Bedrock exposed by tidal scour

Shoreline

Parallel strips of coarse material left by strong tidal currents

Sand deposited in wavy pattern by weaker currents

Irregular patches of fine sand deposited by weakest currents

FEATURES OF THE OCEAN FLOOR

Sediment

Submarine canyon

Continental shelf

Course of mud river

Continental rise

Continental slope

Guyot (flat-topped seamount)

Seamount (underwater mountain)

Abyssal plain

Continental crust

Ooze (sediment consisting of remains of tiny sea creatures)

Layer of volcanic rock

Pillow lava

Volcanic crystalline rock

Oceanic crust

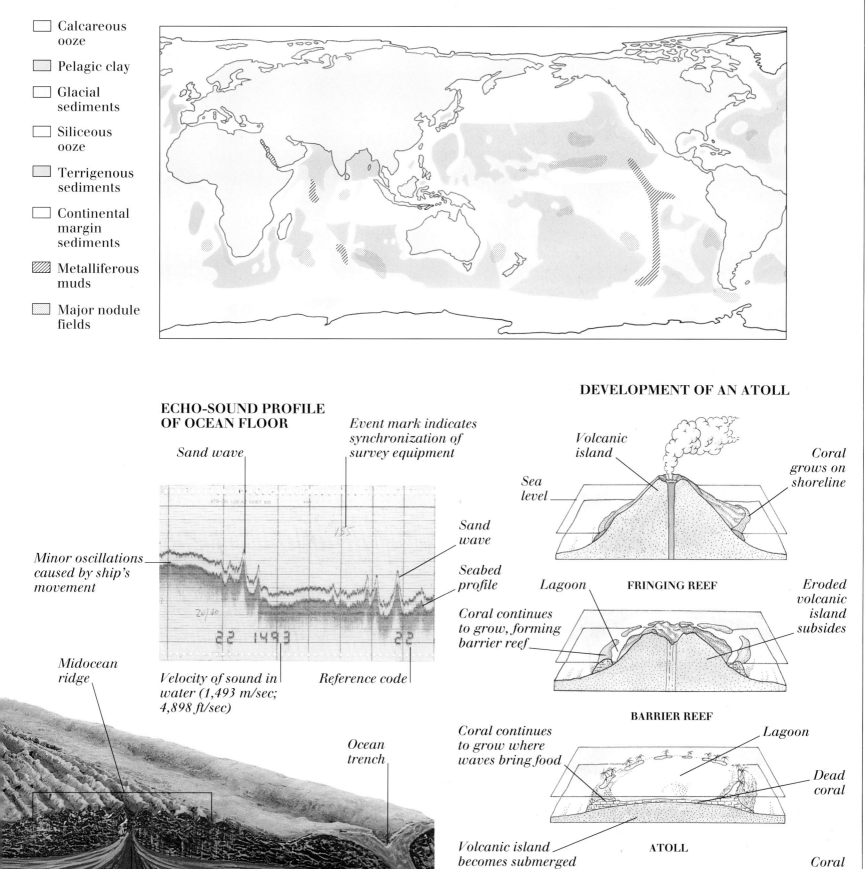

DEEP-OCEAN FLOOR SEDIMENTS

KEY

- ☐ Calcareous ooze
- ☐ Pelagic clay
- ☐ Glacial sediments
- ☐ Siliceous ooze
- ☐ Terrigenous sediments
- ☐ Continental margin sediments
- ▨ Metalliferous muds
- ▦ Major nodule fields

ECHO-SOUND PROFILE OF OCEAN FLOOR

Sand wave

Event mark indicates synchronization of survey equipment

Minor oscillations caused by ship's movement

Sand wave

Seabed profile

Midocean ridge

Velocity of sound in water (1,493 m/sec; 4,898 ft/sec)

Reference code

Ocean trench

Magma (molten rock)

Sediment

DEVELOPMENT OF AN ATOLL

Volcanic island

Sea level

Coral grows on shoreline

FRINGING REEF

Lagoon

Eroded volcanic island subsides

Coral continues to grow, forming barrier reef

BARRIER REEF

Coral continues to grow where waves bring food

Lagoon

Dead coral

Volcanic island becomes submerged

ATOLL

Coral submerged too deeply to grow

Volcanic island is submerged further

SUBMERGED ATOLL

51

The atmosphere

JET STREAM

THE EARTH IS SURROUNDED BY ITS ATMOSPHERE, a blanket of gases that enables life to exist on the planet. This layer has no definite outer edge, gradually becoming thinner until it merges into space, but over 80 percent of atmospheric gases are held by gravity within about 10 miles of the Earth's surface. The atmosphere blocks out much harmful ultraviolet solar radiation, and insulates the Earth against extremes of temperature by limiting both incoming solar radiation and the escape of re-radiated heat into space. This natural balance may be distorted by the greenhouse effect, as gases such as carbon dioxide have built up in the atmosphere, trapping more heat. Close to the Earth's surface, differences in air temperature and pressure cause air to circulate between the equator and poles. This circulation, together with the Coriolis force, gives rise to the prevailing surface winds and the high-level jet streams.

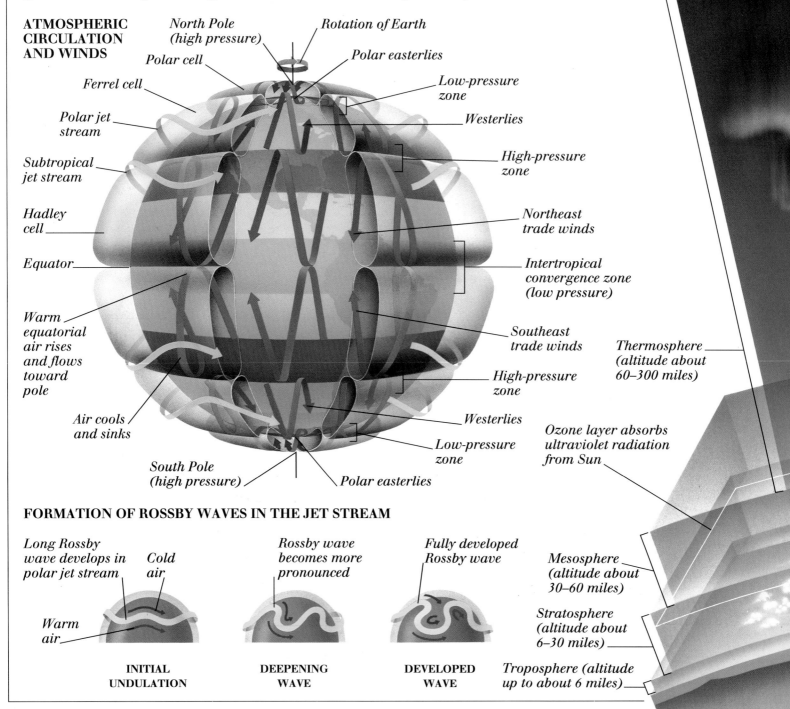

ATMOSPHERIC CIRCULATION AND WINDS

North Pole (high pressure)

Rotation of Earth

Polar cell

Polar easterlies

Ferrel cell

Low-pressure zone

Polar jet stream

Westerlies

Subtropical jet stream

High-pressure zone

Hadley cell

Northeast trade winds

Equator

Intertropical convergence zone (low pressure)

Warm equatorial air rises and flows toward pole

Southeast trade winds

High-pressure zone

Air cools and sinks

Westerlies

Low-pressure zone

South Pole (high pressure)

Polar easterlies

Exosphere (altitude above about 300 miles)

Corona

Thermosphere (altitude about 60–300 miles)

Ozone layer absorbs ultraviolet radiation from Sun

Mesosphere (altitude about 30–60 miles)

Stratosphere (altitude about 6–30 miles)

Troposphere (altitude up to about 6 miles)

FORMATION OF ROSSBY WAVES IN THE JET STREAM

Long Rossby wave develops in polar jet stream

Cold air

Rossby wave becomes more pronounced

Fully developed Rossby wave

Warm air

INITIAL UNDULATION

DEEPENING WAVE

DEVELOPED WAVE

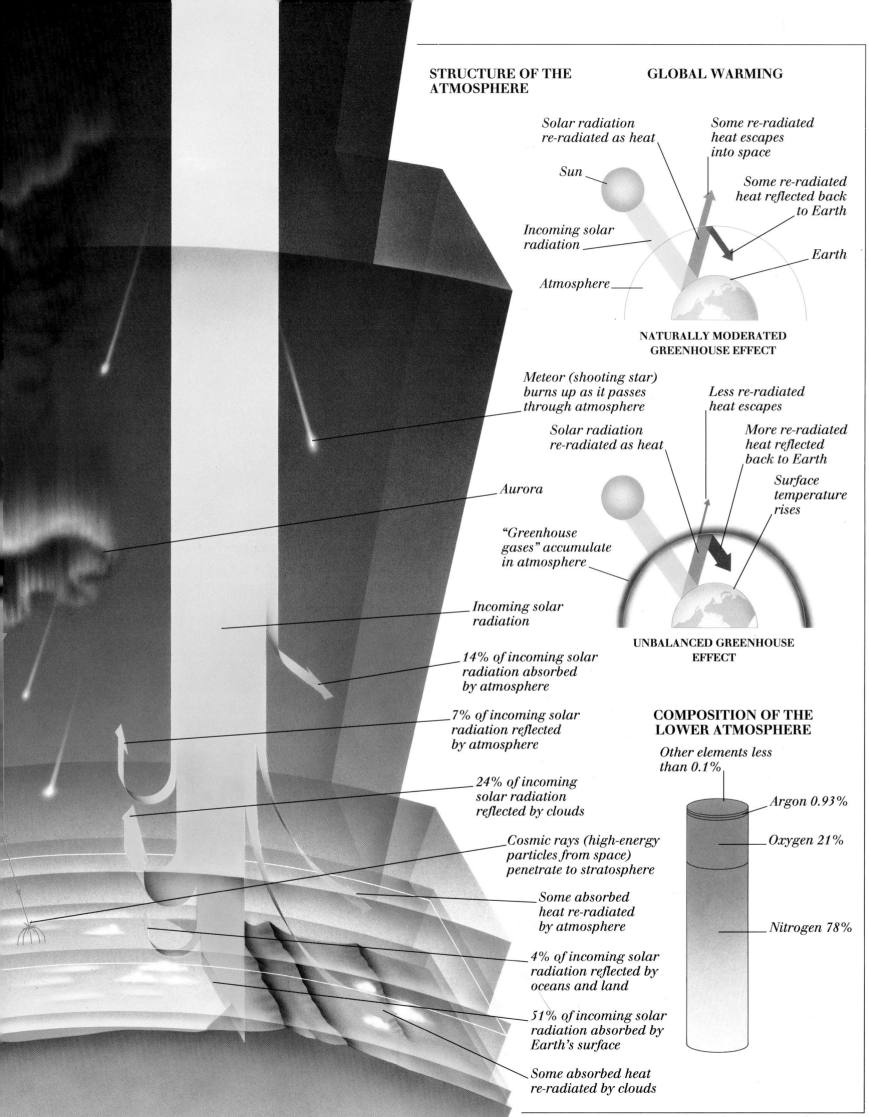

STRUCTURE OF THE ATMOSPHERE

GLOBAL WARMING

Solar radiation re-radiated as heat

Some re-radiated heat escapes into space

Sun

Some re-radiated heat reflected back to Earth

Incoming solar radiation

Earth

Atmosphere

NATURALLY MODERATED GREENHOUSE EFFECT

Meteor (shooting star) burns up as it passes through atmosphere

Less re-radiated heat escapes

Solar radiation re-radiated as heat

More re-radiated heat reflected back to Earth

Aurora

Surface temperature rises

"Greenhouse gases" accumulate in atmosphere

Incoming solar radiation

UNBALANCED GREENHOUSE EFFECT

14% of incoming solar radiation absorbed by atmosphere

7% of incoming solar radiation reflected by atmosphere

COMPOSITION OF THE LOWER ATMOSPHERE

24% of incoming solar radiation reflected by clouds

Other elements less than 0.1%

Argon 0.93%

Cosmic rays (high-energy particles from space) penetrate to stratosphere

Oxygen 21%

Some absorbed heat re-radiated by atmosphere

4% of incoming solar radiation reflected by oceans and land

Nitrogen 78%

51% of incoming solar radiation absorbed by Earth's surface

Some absorbed heat re-radiated by clouds

Weather

WEATHER IS DEFINED AS THE ATMOSPHERIC CONDITIONS at a particular time and place; climate is the average weather conditions for a given region over time. Weather conditions include temperature, wind, cloud cover, and precipitation, such as rain or snow. Good weather is associated with high-pressure areas, where air is sinking. Cloudy, wet, changeable weather is common in low-pressure zones with rising, unstable air. Such conditions occur at temperate latitudes, where warm air meets cool air along the polar fronts. Here, spiraling low-pressure cells known as depressions (mid-latitude cyclones) often form. A depression usually contains a sector of warmer air, beginning at a warm front and ending at a cold front. If the two fronts merge, forming an occluded front, the warm air is pushed upward. An extreme form of low-pressure cell is a hurricane (also called a typhoon or tropical cyclone), which brings torrential rain, and exceptionally strong winds.

TYPES OF CLOUD

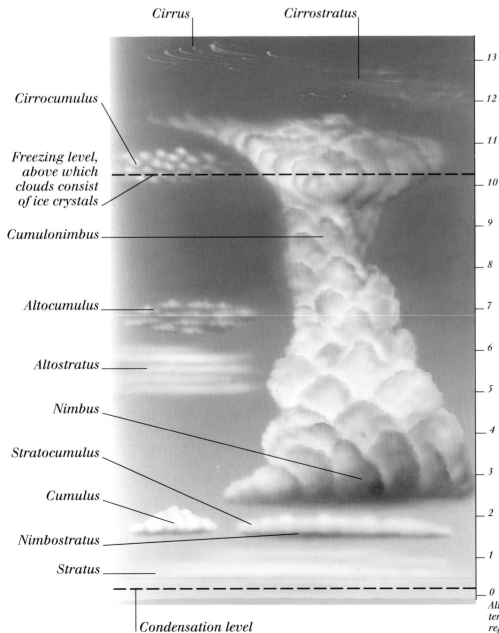

Cirrus

Cirrostratus

Cirrocumulus

Freezing level, above which clouds consist of ice crystals

Cumulonimbus

Altocumulus

Altostratus

Nimbus

Stratocumulus

Cumulus

Nimbostratus

Stratus

Condensation level

13
12
11
10
9
8
7
6
5
4
3
2
1
0

Altitude in temperate regions (km)

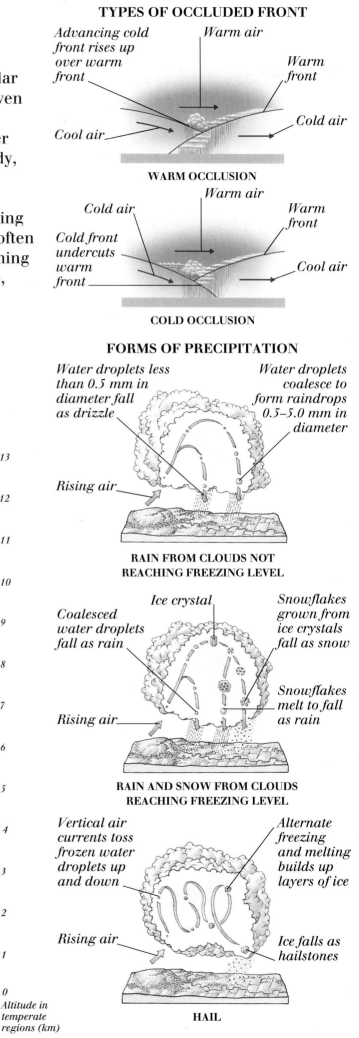

TYPES OF OCCLUDED FRONT

Advancing cold front rises up over warm front

Warm air

Warm front

Cool air

Cold air

WARM OCCLUSION

Cold air

Warm air

Cold front undercuts warm front

Warm front

Cool air

COLD OCCLUSION

FORMS OF PRECIPITATION

Water droplets less than 0.5 mm in diameter fall as drizzle

Water droplets coalesce to form raindrops 0.5–5.0 mm in diameter

Rising air

RAIN FROM CLOUDS NOT REACHING FREEZING LEVEL

Coalesced water droplets fall as rain

Ice crystal

Snowflakes grown from ice crystals fall as snow

Rising air

Snowflakes melt to fall as rain

RAIN AND SNOW FROM CLOUDS REACHING FREEZING LEVEL

Vertical air currents toss frozen water droplets up and down

Alternate freezing and melting builds up layers of ice

Rising air

Ice falls as hailstones

HAIL

STRUCTURE OF A HURRICANE

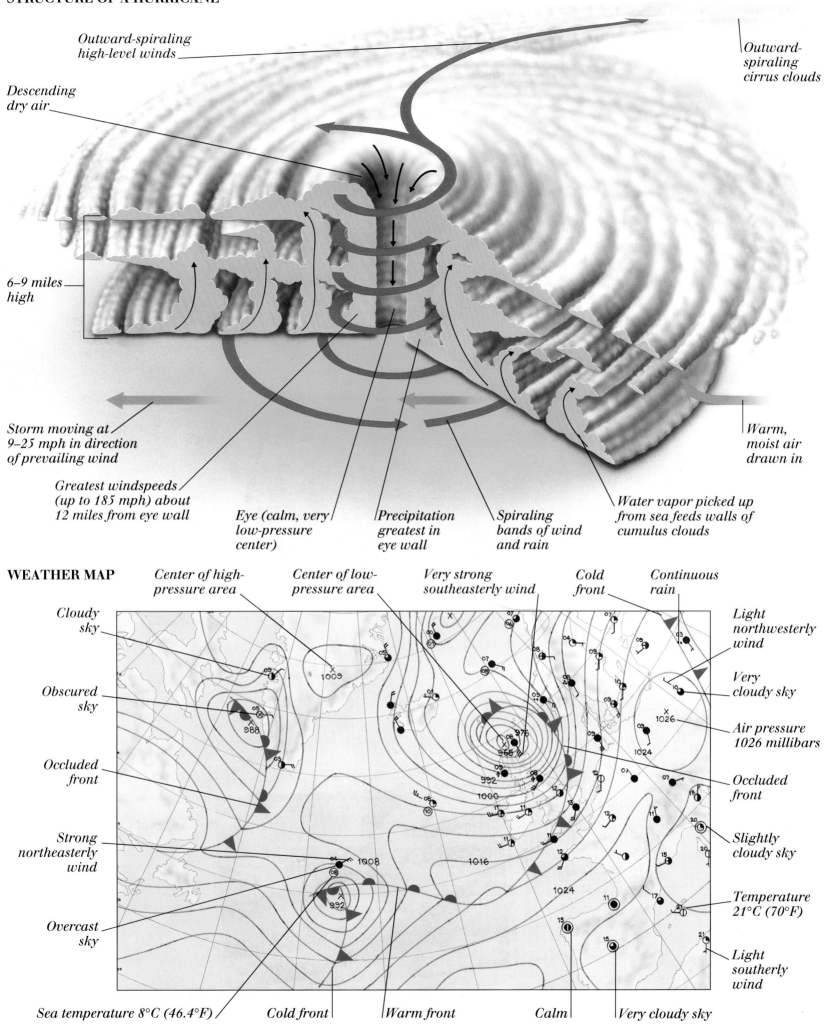

Outward-spiraling
high-level winds

Outward-
spiraling
cirrus clouds

Descending
dry air

6–9 miles
high

Storm moving at
9–25 mph in direction
of prevailing wind

Warm,
moist air
drawn in

Greatest windspeeds
(up to 185 mph) about
12 miles from eye wall

Eye (calm, very
low-pressure
center)

Precipitation
greatest in
eye wall

Spiraling
bands of wind
and rain

Water vapor picked up
from sea feeds walls of
cumulus clouds

WEATHER MAP

Center of high-
pressure area

Center of low-
pressure area

Very strong
southeasterly wind

Cold
Front

Continuous
rain

Cloudy
sky

Light
northwesterly
wind

Obscured
sky

Very
cloudy sky

Occluded
front

Air pressure
1026 millibars

Occluded
front

Strong
northeasterly
wind

Slightly
cloudy sky

Temperature
21°C (70°F)

Overcast
sky

Light
southerly
wind

Sea temperature 8°C (46.4°F)

Cold front

Warm front

Calm

Very cloudy sky

Earth data

EARTH PROFILE

Average distance from Sun (miles)	93,000,000
Maximum distance from Sun (miles)	94,500,000
Minimum distance from Sun (miles)	91,400,000
Length of year (days)	365.26
Length of day (hours)	23.93
Surface temperature range (°F)	-126.9 to 136.4
Mass (billion billion metric tonnes)	5,976
Volume (cu. miles)	259,880,000,000
Axial tilt (degrees)	23.5
Specific gravity (water = 1)	5.52
Polar diameter (miles)	7,900
Equatorial diameter (miles)	7,926
Polar circumference (miles)	24,860
Equatorial circumference (miles)	24,901
Total surface area (sq. miles)	196,900,000
Land surface area (sq. miles)	57,500,000
Land as % of total surface area	29.2
Water surface area (sq. miles)	139,400,000
Water as % of total surface area	70.8
Highest point on land (ft)	29,029
Lowest point on land (ft below sea level)	1,312
Average height of land (ft)	2,756
Greatest ocean depth (ft)	35,840
Average ocean depth (ft)	12,493
Oceanic crust thickness (miles)	4
Continental crust thickness (miles)	25
Mantle thickness (miles)	1,700
Outer core thickness (miles)	1,400
Inner core diameter (miles)	1,500
Approximate age of Earth (millions of years)	4,600

OCEANS AND SEAS

LARGEST AND DEEPEST

Name	Area (sq. miles)	Average depth (ft)
Pacific Ocean	64,186,000	13,215
Atlantic Ocean	33,420,000	12,881
Indian Ocean	28,350,000	13,002
Arctic Ocean	5,106,000	3,953
South China Sea	1,149,000	5,420
Caribbean Sea	972,000	8,093
Mediterranean Sea	969,000	4,688
Bering Sea	873,000	5,075
Gulf of Mexico	582,000	4,875
Sea of Okhotsk	537,000	2,756
Sea of Japan	391,000	4,495
Hudson Bay	282,000	394
East China Sea	257,000	590
Black Sea	196,000	3,609
Red Sea	175,000	1,607
North Sea	165,000	295

DEEP SEA TRENCHES

	Length (miles)	Deepest point	Depth (ft)
Mariana Trench (W. Pacific)	1,398	Challenger Deep	35,840
Tonga-Kermadec Trench (S. Pacific)	1,600	Vityaz II (Tonga)	35,433
Kuril-Kamchatka Trench (W. Pacific)	1,398	Unnamed	34,586
Philippine Trench (W. Pacific)	823	Galathea Deep	34,577
Solomon/New Britain Trench (S. Pacific)	398	Unnamed	29,330
Puerto Rico Trench (W. Atlantic)	497	Milwaukee Deep	28,231
Yap Trench (W. Pacific)	348	Unnamed	27,976
Japan Trench (W. Pacific)	994	Unnamed	27,598
South Sandwich Trench (S. Atlantic)	600	Meteor Deep	27,313

CONTINENTS

Name	Area (sq. miles)	% of total surface area	% of total land area	Highest point	Height (ft)	Lowest point	Below sea level (ft)
Asia	16,980,000	8.6	29.5	Mt. Everest	29,029	Dead Sea	1,312
Africa	11,580,000	5.9	20.1	Kilimanjaro	19,340	Lac Assal	512
N. America	9,260,000	4.7	16.1	Denali (Mt. McKinley)	20,321	Death Valley	282
S. America	6,940,000	3.5	12.1	Aconcagua	22,834	Peninsular Valdez	131
Antarctica	5,400,000	2.7	9.4	Vinson Massif	16,863	Bently Subglacial Trench	8,327
Europe	3,860,000	2.0	6.7	El'brus	18,510	Caspian Sea	92
Australasia	3,480,000	1.8	6.1	Mt. Wilhelm	16,023	Lake Eyre	52

ISLANDS

LARGEST

Name	Area (sq. miles)
Greenland	839,918
New Guinea	306,006
Borneo	280,105
Madagascar	226,662
Baffin Island (Canada)	195,931
Sumatra	165,003
Honshu (Japan)	87,806
Great Britain	84,201
Victoria Island (Canada)	83,896
Ellesmere Island (Canada)	75,768

LAKES AND INLAND SEAS

LARGEST

Name	Area (sq. miles)
Caspian Sea (Asia/Europe)	143,247
Lake Superior (N. America)	31,701
Lake Victoria (Africa)	26,828
Aral Sea (Asia)	24,905
Lake Huron (N. America)	23,000
Lake Michigan (N. America)	22,301
Lake Tanganyika (Africa)	12,700
Lake Baikal (Asia)	12,162
Great Bear Lake (N. America)	12,046
Lake Nyasa (Africa)	11,150

MOUNTAINS

	Name	Height (ft)
HIGHEST	Mt. Everest (Tibet/Nepal)	29,029
	K2 (Pakistan/Tibet)	28,251
	Kangchenjunga (India/Nepal)	28,208
	Makalu (Tibet/Nepal)	27,821
	Cho Oyu (Tibet/Nepal)	26,906
	Dhaulagiri (Nepal)	26,811
	Nanga Parbat (India)	26,660
	Annapurna (Nepal)	26,502
	Gasherbrum (India)	26,470
	Xixabangma Feng (Tibet)	26,290

RIVERS

	Name	Length (miles)
LONGEST	River Nile (Africa)	4,160
	Amazon River (S. America)	4,000
	Yangtze River/Chang Jiang (Asia)	3,964
	Mississippi-Missouri River (N. America)	3,892
	River Ob-Irtysh (Asia)	3,362
	Yellow River/Huang He (Asia)	2,903
	River Congo/Zaire (Africa)	2,900
	River Amur (Asia)	2,744
	River Lena (Asia)	2,734
	Mackenzie-Peace River (N. America)	2,635

WATERFALLS

	Name	Height (ft)
HIGHEST DROP	Angel Falls (Venezuela)	3,212
	Tugela Falls (South Africa)	2,798
	Utgaard (Norway)	2,624
	Mongefossen (Norway)	2,539
	Yosemite Falls (USA)	2,424
	Mardalsfossen (Norway)	2,149
	Cuquenan Falls (Venezuela)	2,001
	Sutherland Falls (New Zealand)	1,903
	Ribbon Falls (USA)	1,611
	Gavarnie (France)	1,384

	Name	Volume (cu. ft/sec)
GREATEST VOLUME	Boyoma Falls (Zaire)	600
	Guaira Falls (Brazil/Paraguay)	459
	Khone Falls (Laos)	406
	Niagara Falls (Canada/USA)	212
	Paulo Afonso Falls (Brazil)	99
	Urubupunga Falls (Brazil)	95
	Cataras del Iguazu Falls (Brazil/Paraguay)	60
	Patos-Maribondo Falls (Brazil)	53
	Victoria Falls (Zimbabwe)	39
	Churchill Falls (Canada)	35

ACTIVE VOLCANOES

	Name	Height (ft)
HIGHEST	Guallatiri (Chile)	19,882
	Lascar (Chile)	19,652
	Cotopaxi (Ecuador)	19,642
	Tupungatito (Chile)	18,503
	Ruiz (Colombia)	17,716
	Sangay (Ecuador)	17,159
	Purace (Colombia)	15,600
	Klyuchevskaya Sopka (Russia)	15,584
	Colima (Mexico)	14,002
	Galeras (Colombia)	13,996

DESERTS

	Name	Area (sq. miles)
LARGEST	Sahara (Africa)	3,398,000
	Gobi Desert (Asia)	502,000
	Australian Desert (Australasia)	483,000
	Arabian Desert (Asia)	328,000
	Kalahari Desert (Africa)	224,000
	Chihuahuan Desert (N. America)	143,000
	Takla Makan Desert (Asia)	124,000
	Kara Kum (Asia)	120,000
	Namib Desert (Africa)	120,000
	Thar Desert (Asia)	100,000

CAVES

	Name	Depth (ft)
DEEPEST	Reseau Jean Bernard (France)	5,256
	Shakta Pantjukhina (Georgia)	4,948
	Lamrechtsofen (Austria)	4,872
	Sistema del Trave (Spain)	4,728
	Boj Bulok (Uzbekistan)	4,642

	Name	Length (miles)
LONGEST SYSTEMS	Mammoth Cave System (USA)	348
	Optimisticheskaya (Ukraine)	114
	Hölloch (Switzerland)	85
	Jewel Cave (USA)	79
	Ozernaya (Ukraine)	66

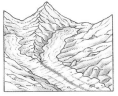

GLACIERS

	Name	Length (miles)
LONGEST	Lambert-Fisher Ice Passage (Antarctica)	320
	Novaya Zemlya (Russia)	260
	Arctic Institute Ice Passage (Antarctica)	225
	Nimrod-Lennox-King Ice Passage (Antarctica)	179
	Denman Glacier (Antarctica)	150
	Beardmore Glacier (Antarctica)	140
	Recovery Glacier (Antarctica)	140
	Petermanns Gletscher (Greenland)	124
	Unnamed glacier (Antarctica)	120
	Slessor Glacier (Antarctica)	115

WEATHER

Records

Highest recorded temperature:
  136.4°F at Al' Aziziyah, Libya, 13 September 1922.
Lowest recorded temperature:
  -126.9°F at Vostok, Antarctica, 24 August 1960.
Greatest average yearly rainfall:
  451 inches at Mt. Wai'ale'ale, Hawaii.
Greatest recorded rainfall in any one year:
  1,048 inches at Cherrapunji, India, in 1860–61.
Windiest place:
  Commonwealth Bay, Antarctica, where several
  199 mph winds occur each year.
Highest recorded windspeed:
  230 mph on Mt. Washington, USA, in 1934.

WINDSPEED

	No.	Description	Speed (mph)	Characteristics
BEAUFORT SCALE	0	Calm	Below 1	Smoke rises vertically.
	1	Light air	1–3	Smoke blown by wind.
	2	Light breeze	4–7	Leaves rustle.
	3	Gentle breeze	8–12	Extends a light flag.
	4	Moderate breeze	13–18	Raises dust and loose paper.
	5	Fresh breeze	19–24	Small trees begin to sway.
	6	Strong breeze	25–31	Large branches in motion.
	7	Near gale	32–38	Whole trees in motion.
	8	Gale	39–46	Twigs broken off trees.
	9	Strong gale	47–54	Structural damage occurs.
	10	Storm	55–63	Trees uprooted.
	11	Violent storm	64–72	Widespread damage.
	12–17	Hurricane	Over 75	Extremely violent.

EARTHQUAKES

	Magnitude	Probable effects
RICHTER SCALE	1	Detectable only by instruments.
	2–2.5	Barely detectable even near epicenter.
	4–5	Detectable within 20 miles of epicenter; may cause slight damage.
	6	Moderately destructive.
	7	A major earthquake.
	8–9	A very destructive earthquake.

CHEMICAL ELEMENTS

●	Ac	Actinium	● Mn	Manganese
●	Ag	Silver	● Mo	Molybdenum
○	Al	Aluminum	N	Nitrogen
●	Am	Americium	● Na	Sodium
●	Ar	Argon	● Nb	Niobium
○	As	Arsenic	● Nd	Neodymium
○	At	Astatine	● Ne	Neon
●	Au	Gold	● Ni	Nickel
●	B	Boron	● No	Nobelium
●	Ba	Barium	● Np	Neptunium
●	Be	Beryllium	● O	Oxygen
○	Bi	Bismuth	● Os	Osmium
●	Bk	Berkelium	● P	Phosphorus
○	Br	Bromine	● Pa	Protactinium
○	C	Carbon	● Pb	Lead
●	Ca	Calcium	● Pd	Palladium
●	Cd	Cadmium	● Pm	Promethium
●	Ce	Cerium	○ Po	Polonium
○	Cf	Californium	● Pr	Praseodymium
○	Cl	Chlorine	● Pt	Platinum
●	Cm	Curium	● Pu	Plutonium
●	Co	Cobalt	● Ra	Radium
●	Cr	Chromium	● Rb	Rubidium
○	Cs	Cesium	● Re	Rhenium
●	Cu	Copper	● Rf-Ku	Rutherfordium-Kurchatovium
○	Dy	Dysprosium		
●	Er	Erbium	● Rh	Rhodium
○	Es	Einsteinium	● Rn	Radon
●	Eu	Europium	● Ru	Ruthenium
○	F	Fluorine	○ S	Sulfur
●	Fe	Iron	○ Sb	Antimony
●	Fm	Fermium	● Sc	Scandium
●	Fr	Francium	○ Se	Selenium
○	Ga	Gallium	○ Si	Silicon
●	Gd	Gadolinium	● Sm	Samarium
○	Ge	Germanium	○ Sn	Tin
●	H	Hydrogen	● Sr	Strontium
●	Ha	Hahnium	● Ta	Tantalum
●	He	Helium	● Tb	Terbium
●	Hf	Hafnium	● Tc	Technetium
●	Hg	Mercury	○ Te	Tellurium
○	Ho	Holmium	● Th	Thorium
○	I	Iodine	● Ti	Titanium
○	In	Indium	○ Tl	Thallium
●	Ir	Iridium	● Tm	Thulium
●	K	Potassium	○ U	Uranium
●	Kr	Krypton	● V	Vanadium
●	La	Lanthanum	● W	Tungsten
●	Li	Lithium	● Xe	Xenon
●	Lr	Lawrencium	● Y	Yttrium
●	Lu	Lutetium	● Yb	Ytterbium
●	Md	Mendelevium	● Zn	Zinc
●	Mg	Magnesium	● Zr	Zirconium

● Alkaline earth metals	● Lanthanide series
● Alkali metals	● Actinide series
○ Other metals	● Nonmetals
● Transition metals	● Noble gases

● Hydrogen is a gas with unique properties and is therefore usually placed in a group by itself.

Glossary

AQUIFER: A layer of water-saturated permeable rock lying on a layer of impermeable rock. It can be a source of water for wells and springs.

ARTESIAN BASIN: An aquifer in which water is held under pressure between two layers of impermeable rock. (See also Aquifer.)

ASTHENOSPHERE: A partly molten layer of the Earth's mantle below the lithosphere. (See also Lithosphere; Mantle.)

ATMOSPHERE: The layer of gases surrounding the Earth, consisting of (from ground level upward) the troposphere, stratosphere, mesosphere, thermosphere, and exosphere.

BATHOLITH: A large, domed, igneous intrusion composed of granitic rock.

BED: A layer or stratum of rock (usually sedimentary). A **competent bed** is one liable to break under stress. An **incompetent bed** is one liable to bend or flow under stress.

CALDERA: A basin-shaped volcanic depression, typically resulting from an eruption and/or collapse of a volcano.

CLEAVAGE: The tendency of a mineral to break along well-defined planes of weakness.

CLIMATE: The average weather conditions for a region over a long period of time. (See also Weather.)

CONTINENTAL DRIFT: The theory that today's continents were formed by the breakup of prehistoric supercontinents that have slowly drifted to their present positions. (See also Plate tectonics.)

CORE: The central portion of the Earth, made up of a solid inner core and a molten outer core.

CORIOLIS FORCE: A force that results from the Earth's rotation. It deflects winds and water to the right in the Northern Hemisphere and to the left in the Southern Hemisphere.

CRUST: The outer layer of the Earth lying above the mantle. There are two main types: continental and oceanic crust.

CRYSTAL: A geometric form of a mineral, with naturally formed plane faces that reflect the arrangement of its constituent atoms.

DESERT: An arid region where precipitation is generally less than 10 inches per year.

EARTHQUAKE: Shock waves, sometimes causing violent tremors at the Earth's surface, caused in most cases by sudden crustal displacement along a fault. (See also Epicenter; Focus.)

ELEMENT: A substance that cannot be broken down by chemical means into simpler substances.

EON: A division of geological time that can be subdivided into eras (see Era).

EPICENTER: The point on the Earth's surface directly above the focus of an earthquake. (See also Earthquake; Focus.)

EPOCH: A division of geological time that is a subdivision of a period (see Period).

ERA: A division of geological time that is a subdivision of an eon and which can be subdivided into a period. (See also Eon; Period.)

EROSION: The wearing away and removal of exposed land by water, wind, and/or ice. (See also Weathering.)

EXOSPHERE: The outermost layer of the atmosphere (see Atmosphere).

FAULT: A fracture in a rock along which there may be displacement of one side relative to the other.

FOCUS: The point underground at which an earthquake originates. (See also Earthquake; Epicenter.)

FOLD: A buckle or bend in a rock layer due to horizontal pressure in the Earth's crust. An **anticline** is an arch-shaped fold. A **syncline** is a trough-shaped fold.

FOSSIL: The remains, traces, or impressions of plants and animals that have been preserved in rock.

FRACTURE: The tendency of a mineral or rock to break in an irregular way.

FRONT: The boundary between two air masses. At a **warm front**, warm air rises up over cold air; at a **cold front**, cold air pushes under warm air.

GLACIER: A large mass of ice that forms on land and moves slowly downhill under its own weight.

GREENHOUSE EFFECT: The process in which radiation from the Sun passes through the atmosphere, is reflected and re-radiated from the Earth's surface, and is then trapped by atmospheric gases. The buildup of "greenhouse gases," such as carbon dioxide, has increased the effect, leading to global warming.

GROUNDMASS: The finer-grained material of a rock in which larger crystals or pebbles are embedded. **Matrix** is an alternative term for groundmass.

GROUNDWATER: Water accumulated beneath the Earth's surface.

GUTENBERG DISCONTINUITY: The boundary between the mantle and the outer core.

GYRE: The circular rotation of the waters of the major oceans and seas, driven by winds and the Coriolis force. (See also Coriolis force.)

HABIT: The typical form taken by an aggregate of a mineral's crystals.

IGNEOUS ROCK: A rock that is formed from solidified magma or lava. **Intrusive igneous rocks** are formed underground; **extrusive igneous rocks** are formed on the surface.

LAVA: Molten magma expelled on to the Earth's surface through volcanoes or fissures. The two most common forms in which lava solidifies are known as **aa** (irregular jagged blocks), and **pahoehoe** (rope-like strands).

LITHIFICATION: The formation of rock from unconsolidated sediment by the processes of compression and cementation. (See also Sedimentary rock.)

LITHOSPHERE: The Earth's crust and the topmost layer of the mantle.

LONGSHORE DRIFT: Movement of sand and small rocks along the seashore, driven by the action of waves.

MAGMA: Molten rock originating in the Earth's mantle and crust.

MANTLE: The layer of the Earth between the outer core and the crust.

MESOSPHERE: The layer of the atmosphere above the stratosphere and below the thermosphere. (See also Atmosphere.)

METAMORPHIC ROCK: A rock that is formed from previously existing rocks that have been subjected to intense heat and/or pressure, to the extent that their chemical composition has been altered.

MINERAL: A naturally occurring substance that has a characteristic chemical composition and specific physical properties.

MOHOROVICIC DISCONTINUITY: The boundary between the crust and mantle.

MOHS' SCALE: A scale by which the relative hardness of minerals can be measured.

OROGENESIS: The term used to describe the processes involved in mountain building.

PERIOD: A division of geological time that is a subdivision of an era and which can be subdivided into an epoch. (See also Epoch; Era.)

PLATE TECTONICS: The theory that the Earth's lithosphere consists of several semirigid plates that move relative to each other.

PRECIPITATION: All forms of water particles that fall from clouds, including rain, hail, sleet, and snow.

PYROCLAST: A rock formed from the debris of an explosive volcanic eruption.

ROCK: An aggregate of minerals. Rocks are divided into three main groups: igneous, metamorphic, and sedimentary (see Igneous rock; Metamorphic rock; Sedimentary rock).

ROCK CYCLE: The continuous cycle through which old rocks are transformed into new ones.

SEAFLOOR SPREADING: The process by which new seafloor crust is created at ridges in midocean where two adjacent plates move away from each other. (See also Plate tectonics.)

SEDIMENTARY ROCK: A rock formed by the lithification of sediment. (See also Lithification.)

SPRING: A flow of groundwater that emerges naturally on the Earth's surface.

STRATOSPHERE: The layer of the atmosphere above the troposphere and below the mesosphere. (See also Atmosphere.)

STRATUM: A layer or bed of rock. (See also Bed.)

STREAK: The color that a powdered mineral makes when rubbed across an unglazed tile.

SUBDUCTION ZONE: An area where one plate is forced under another. (See also Plate tectonics.)

THERMOSPHERE: The highest layer of the atmosphere. (See also Atmosphere.)

TIDE: The regular rise and fall of the ocean surface resulting principally from the gravitational forces between the Earth, Moon, and Sun.

TRAP: A folded or faulted layer of impermeable rock beneath which oil and gas may accumulate.

TRENCH: A long, narrow valley on the ocean floor found along a subduction zone. (See also Subduction zone.)

TROPOSPHERE: The lowest layer of the atmosphere. (See also Atmosphere.)

UNCONFORMITY: A major break in a sequence of rock strata that represents a period when no new sediments were being laid down and/or when earlier sedimentary layers were eroded away.

VOLCANO: A vent or fissure in the Earth's crust through which molten magma and hot gases escape. Most volcanoes occur along plate boundaries.

WATER CYCLE: The processes by which water is circulated between land, the oceans, and the atmosphere. An alternative name is the **hydrologic cycle**.

WATER TABLE: The level up to which the ground is permanently saturated.

WEATHER: The atmospheric conditions at a particular time and place. (See also Climate.)

WEATHERING: The breaking down of rocks when they are exposed on the Earth's surface by physical (mechanical) or chemical means. (See also Erosion.)

Index

Acknowledgments

Dorling Kindersley would like to thank:
Dr. John Nudds, The Manchester Museum, Manchester; Dr. Alan Wooley and Dr. Andrew Clark, The Natural History Museum, London; Graham Bartlett, National Meteorological Library and Archive, Bracknell; Tony Drake, BP Exploration, Uxbridge; Jane Davies, Royal Society of Chemistry, Cambridge; Dr. Tony Waltham, Nottingham Trent University, Nottingham; Staff at the Smithsonian Institute, Washington, D.C.; Staff at the United States Geological Survey, Washington, D.C.; Staff at the National Geographic Society, Washington, D.C.; Staff at Edward Lawrence Associates (Export Ltd.), Midhurst; John Farndon; David Lambert

Picture credits:
BP Exploration 51c; Bruce Coleman Ltd/Andy Price 18tl; Robert Harding jacket, 16tl; Hutchison Picture Library 14cl; Nature Photographers/ Paul Sterry 38tl; SPL/ Earth Satellite Corporation 40cl, 45br; Simon Fraser 20tl; NASA 43tr, 52tl; David Parker 17bl; Tom Van Sant 6tl, 8-9c, 19tr, 33tr, 48-49c; Floor of the Oceans, by Bruce C. Heezen and Marie Tharp 1975. © Marie Tharp 1980. Reproduced by permission of Marie Tharp, 1 Washington Ave, South Nyack, NY 10960, USA 13tr; G. Steenmans 44tl; Tony Stone Worldwide 32tl; Zefa/Janicek jacket, 28tl

(t=top, b=bottom, l=left, r=right, c=center)

Picture research:
Christine Rista, Catherine O'Rourke, Anna Lord

Additional editorial assistance:
Emily Hill, Cathy Rubinstein

Additional design assistance:
Sue Knight

Index:
Kay Wright